PRAISE FOR *ASSESSMENT CENTRE SUCCESS*

'At last a practical and insightful guide to making the most of your opportunity at an assessment centre – a must-read.' **Sue Ormerod, Regional Director, Nigel Wright Recruitment**

'I have seen Tony Weightman use many of these techniques and tips with the MBA students I teach and with other groups. These ideas are not only useful in the development of the students' careers but also help them in gaining valuable jobs. This book offers ideas and techniques that are easy to follow and implement.' **Richard Da Costa, MBA Tutor, Newcastle University**

'Tony Weightman will always be my first choice for any HR-related topics, so I am delighted that he has chosen to give advice on how to secure that job you have always dreamed about. Every time I have worked with him, he has delivered and shared his huge experience with good practical examples from the real world – you understand immediately what he is trying to convey. This book is a must on your journey to securing your dream job.' **Carsten Staehr, CEO, Cintra**

'Weightman Associates are for many HR professionals and business leaders the go-to company to partner with in order to ensure bespoke measurable development of employees, line managers and future leaders.

With *Assessment Centre Success*, Tony Weightman has delivered an essential guide that offers practical tips and techniques for achieving success, and that should be in any candidate's toolkit. The book equips the reader with skills and knowledge that will set them apart in the competitive marketplace, so they stand out to employers looking for first-class talent through an assessment centre.' **Gill Usher, HR Manager, Rocket Medical**

'In this book Tony Weightman has distilled many years of experience into an easy-to-read guide that is an essential for anyone preparing for an assessment centre.' **Catherine Attwell FCIPD, HR Director**

ASSESSMENT CENTRE SUCCESS

Your ultimate resource of practice exercises and sample questions to help you ace the activities, beat the competition and impress employers

TONY WEIGHTMAN

KoganPage

First published in Great Britain and the United States in 2018 by Kogan Page Limited

2nd Floor, 45 Gee Street	c/o Martin P Hill Consulting	4737/23 Ansari Road
London	122 W 27th St, 10th Floor	Daryaganj
EC1V 3RS	New York NY 10001	New Delhi 110002
United Kingdom	USA	India

www.koganpage.com

© Tony Weightman, 2018

The right of Tony Weightman to be identified as the author of this work has been asserted by him in accordance with the Copyright, Designs and Patents Act 1988.

ISBN   978 0 7494 8313 5
E-ISBN 978 0 7494 8314 2

British Library Cataloguing-in-Publication Data

A CIP record for this book is available from the British Library.

Library of Congress Cataloging-in-Publication Data

Names: Weightman, Tony, author.
Title: Assessment centre success : your ultimate resource of practice
    exercises and sample questions to help you ace the activities, beat the
    competition and impress employers / Tony Weightman.
Description: London ; New York : Kogan Page, [2018] | Includes
    bibliographical references and index.
Identifiers: LCCN 2018024734 (print) | LCCN 2018026925 (ebook) | ISBN
    9780749483142 (ebook) | ISBN 9780749483135 (pbk.)
Subjects: LCSH: Employment tests–Great Britain. | Employee selection–Great
    Britain.
Classification: LCC HF5549.5.E5 (ebook) | LCC HF5549.5.E5 W445 2018 (print) |
    DDC 658.3/1125–dc23

Typeset by Integra Software Services, Pondicherry
Print production managed by Jellyfish
Printed and bound by CPI Group (UK) Ltd, Croydon, CR0 4YY

This book is dedicated to my wife Tracey, who has offered unlimited support during its writing.

Tracey, you were always there when I needed a break or a person to bounce ideas off.

I thank you for your support and understanding. You will never know how much I valued your input and counsel.

CONTENTS

ABOUT THE AUTHOR

Tony Weightman has over 30 years' experience as a consultant in Human Resources for organizations as diverse as GSK, Nestlé, Virgin Atlantic, Nissan and Transport for London. He is degree educated in Business Studies, is a fellow of CIPD and has been Chair of the local CIPD branch committee.

He has developed and run assessment centres for some of the largest organizations in the UK, including organizations in manufacturing, engineering, hotels and catering, as well as in the charity sector. He has most recently been commissioned to work with a major university to design an assessment centre for use by MBA students prior to the completion of their course, to enable them to better fit into the world of work. Tony has a practical approach that has been used to coach many people to prepare for assessment events.

His early career was with Procter & Gamble, Unilever, and Scottish and Newcastle Breweries. He has held posts in Production and Human Resources and has operated at board level for most of his working life.

Outside work, Tony has been active in Rugby Union, mainly as a player, but has also been President of his local club. He is an avid reader and now plays golf mainly for fun.

If you have any comments about the book or want to share your experiences of assessment centres you can contact Tony at Tonyw8@talktalk.net

ACKNOWLEDGEMENTS

First and foremost I must thank Rebecca Bush, the editor of this book, for her fantastic input and being able to offer such great advice. I will always be thankful for the time and thought you gave to this book and the encouragement you have given me to express myself as an author.

There are four people in my life who have helped to build my confidence and skill as a person. My father, Thomas, was a great inspiration due to his intellect and knowledge. I can only thank him for his support and the fact that he backed my every decision in life without either criticism or scorn. God rest his soul. The other three are people who developed my confidence at school and college. Paddy Powell and John Wade turned me from a person who lacked confidence and vision into a person who was free to develop both intellectual and sporting confidence. Finally, Eric Wade was perhaps the best tutor I could have been given at college. Not only did he encourage me to grow as a person, he was also a great role model.

I would like to formally thank my great friends, the famous four who offered support for the writing of the book. Richard DaCosta, Phil Atkinson, Nigel Mason and Gareth Williams all kept a close eye on my progress and were willing ears to any ideas I had. They were all there if I needed help and were present for our Friday night get-togethers.

My best pal Adrian Jackson will never know how helpful he has been during the writing process. Not only is he a great friend, he is the best devil's advocate I know. He can always see the alternative side of an argument. I will be forever grateful for that type of input, as well as for his great humour when it was necessary.

Bernie McCardle and I are writing a book together at the moment. He offered support at all stages of this book and understood the dilemma I often faced when trying to write two books at the same time.

I must offer a great amount of thanks to John Grant, who is a most valued colleague at Weightman Associates. This is a practical person who has helped ensure the examples were represented properly and the content made sense. He offered all manner of support and ideas for this book.

Introduction

The first assessment centre I attended was a complete mystery to me. I had no idea what to expect and did not understand why I was required for two days. All my friends had different tales about what to expect based on their own experiences and, in some cases, mere speculation – in fact, everyone I talked to had a different perspective on the format of the event.

I tried to approach it with an open mind but was still very uncomfortable about not knowing what would happen. However, at the start of the first day, the person responsible for the event explained what we would be doing and why they were using these different approaches. They took their time to explain and answer any relevant questions, and by the end I was much more at ease and ready to take part in the event.

I did not get that particular job in the end, but what I did get was valuable experience that helped me in future job quests. I was no longer afraid of the assessment centre approach; it was no longer a mystery, and was in fact rather practical and at times even fun. Since then, having taken part in, designed, run, and consulted on many assessment centres for a broad range of industries, I have never encountered the same approach in two different organizations, and more and more are using this tool to recruit the best talent available and ensure the candidates meet the required standards to be successful in the role – and that growth will increase even more as the skills gap increases in the UK.

In *Assessment Centre Success* we will look at the reasons assessment centres are used and how they are structured, enabling you to build your confidence rather than feeling like you are going into the unknown, because you will be aware of what the organization expects from you. You will be shown how to prepare and how to identify the types of exercises that will be used at the event. Time will be spent on creating and maintaining the positive impression you wish to make on the assessors.

You will see a number of real examples of exercises that have been used by various employers when running their assessment processes. Each exercise will be explained in a practical manner to make it easier for you to understand what is required. We will explain what the employer is looking for from the exercise and why it is important to the process; when you are aware of these things you can ensure you are focusing your efforts in the right direction. Time will be spent showing you how to tackle each type of exercise in order to complete it correctly and achieve success. You will be given a number of relevant tips and techniques to employ to ensure you are seen by the employer as a credible candidate. Where appropriate, there will be a template or model that you can use to practise the exercise so you feel really prepared. We will cover both individual and group-type exercises, showing you the variety of approaches organizations can take, and you will be given general guidance to apply to each exercise to ensure you know what you are doing and what is required by the assessor.

To back up your assessment centre performance. there is also advice to help you perform at your best during the one-to-one interview, focusing on the required job skills and knowledge that you will have identified previously. Appropriate time will be spent on the process of both asking and answering questions in the interview.

We will also look at some typical worries many candidates will have and identify how best to make a positive impact in these situations, with some easy-to-follow guidance to help you even if mistakes have happened. This should assist you in taking the worry out of what can be a difficult and stressful situation.

How to use this book

You can engage with this book in many different ways in order to get what you want from it. You can use the standard approach of reading from page one to the end, which will be most useful to those who have little or no experience of the assessment process. By doing this you will gradually build your confidence and knowledge, and will ensure you get the most from the book.

If you have more experience you may be able to identify the chapters most relevant for assisting with your preparation, and scan the rest of the book. For example, maybe you are already confident with face-to-face interviews so will rather want to focus on the practical exercises in Chapters 5, 6 and 7. Or maybe you want to particularly focus on how to get the best out of your feedback by using the tools in Chapter 11.

Once you have read the book you can then use it as a reminder or guide for when you next face an assessment process, helping you to build on your own relevant experience and review what has worked and not worked in the past. It will aid you with new ideas and approaches for your next assessment centre.

I wish you every success in taking part in the assessment process, and I hope this book will help you build your confidence for when you next encounter an assessment event. Remember, you need to prepare well for any event you take part in, so that you gain the success you require. Success only comes from hard and applied work; let that hard work and application start now.

01
What is an assessment centre?

Most people will not know what an assessment centre is or what it is designed to do, yet they are now an integral part of the recruitment process used by many organizations if they are serious about getting the best employees. Many surveys have found that the interview process as a solo tool is not very effective in predicting those candidates that will fulfil the needs of the vacant role – in fact, interviews alone are seen as only around 10 per cent reliable in predicting a successful candidate (Dale, 2005).

I have been developing and managing the hiring process as well as advising some of the largest organizations in the UK on how to hire effectively for 35 years now, and in my experience, organizations need to take a more practical approach to recruitment in order to get better results. Such results will show that employees hired through an in-depth, practical approach are more likely to be well suited to the role and will probably stay in the organization longer, which is a great benefit when you consider the cost of recruitment and the cost of a failed new employee. An assessment centre will offer that practical approach – let's look at how.

What is it?

An assessment centre is an approach to recruitment that tests the skills and behaviour of the candidate against the requirements of the job. It will not rely purely on an interview where you traditionally tell the interviewer about your skills and they have to take your word for it. The assessment centre will actually test these skills using various exercises and validated tests. In this way, the recruiting organization gets to see how you work, rather than only hearing how you say you work. It is this practical element that is so popular with recruiters.

If you look back at your life, you will find that you have more experience of assessments than you perhaps had realized. At school, some of the topics you covered had a practical element to the exam; for example, physics, chemistry or engineering have practical exercises as part of the A Level exam, to establish if you can relate the theory into practice in a safe and structured manner. In team sports such as rugby, hockey and football you may have been involved in trial matches to establish how you coped in a real match situation, and in solo sports such as judo, you might have passed through the grading system of belts not only by knowing the theory, but by being able to demonstrate it on the judo mat in a formal grading event. As an adult, anyone who can drive a car will be well aware of the driving test; a practical and a theory test of your skills and ability. The practical test takes the learner onto the roads in a real situation and enables the assessor to establish if they are safe to drive a car on the roads, while the theory test establishes if they have the knowledge to engage a car safely on the roads.

Whether or not we were aware of it at the time, all of the above are examples of forms of assessment centre, as they test skills, knowledge and behaviour. We just take them as a normal part of what we do in our lives, because they are well-established approaches that are understood by most people.

Despite this, the word 'assessment' will usually strike some level of fear into most people. We – understandably – do not usually welcome the idea that someone we don't know will assess us. The main concern most people seem to have is that the assessor does not know you and therefore only has a limited view of what you can do. This may be true; however, an assessment takes place whenever we meet new people in any walk of life. We naturally determine if they are a person we want to meet again or not. We may not call it assessment, but it is a form of assessment based on what we observe about the person and how they behave and act. The level of assessment may be based on only one aspect of the person but we regard our assessment as relevant at the time. Over time we get to know the person better – from what we observe. All too often, our first impressions are misplaced due to focusing on only one aspect of our meeting. The assessment centre overcomes this as it looks at the total person and does not draw any conclusions from just one exercise or aspect of the process – it is much more thorough.

Why are they used?

As mentioned above, employers use the assessment centre as a means to identify whether candidates meet set criteria for a particular role. They use a series of practical exercises to observe the skills and behaviours of candidates, get a practical view of how you work, and identify how closely you match the needs of the job and the organization.

Cost

Too many organizations have spent large sums of money on their recruitment endeavours (Figure 1.1) only to find that it was wasted because the candidate did not fit with the role or the organization.

Figure 1.1 Cost of recruitment

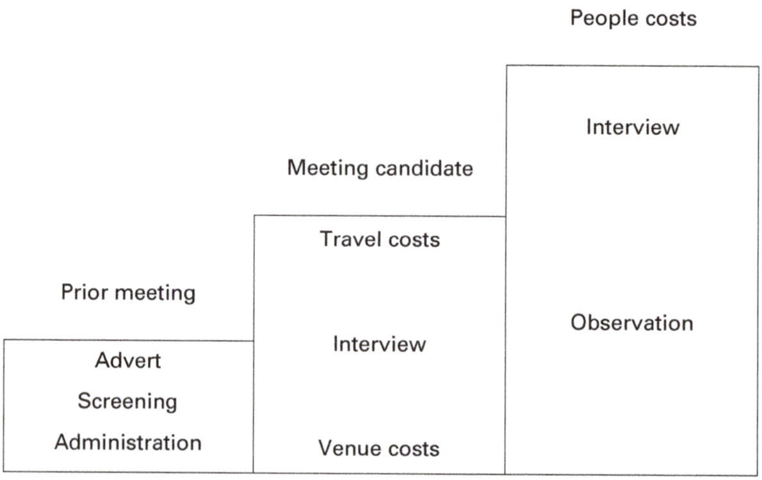

People costs

Interview

Meeting candidate

Travel costs

Prior meeting

Observation

Advert

Interview

Screening

Administration

Venue costs

This failure has a huge impact on the morale of current employees as well as on the new staff member's stress levels. Then, if the new employee fails to remain with the organization, the company may be dealing with a dent in their brand, which they have been developing over many years, as well as the financial cost to the organization as they have to go about the recruitment again (Figure 1.2). They will incur the advertising or agency costs as well as their own time spent in the recruitment process. The cost of an induction programme, too, is heavy on individual costs, as staff are taken away from their normal roles.

Figure 1.2   Cost of failure

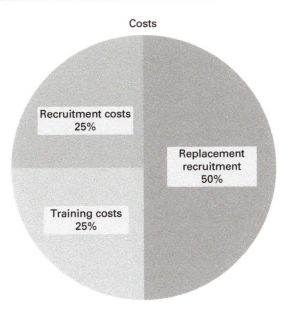

In addition to the costs of failure, there is another potential cost; even if the employee is not a good fit for the organization or the job, they may decide to remain and just tick over instead of leaving. Such people can be disruptive and may cause problems for their colleagues, along with the fact that the value they add to the company fails to outweigh the cost of their ongoing salary and benefits.

This is why organizations have been carefully considering how best to get the employees they want. It is not easy to develop and use an assessment process; it can be very expensive to run, as it involves a lot of people. However, as we can see, the benefits do outweigh the costs.

Finding the best candidate

Putting the costs to one side, organizations are looking to identify the best fit for the job. By using practical exercises that relate to their organization, they can observe how someone will react and work. The assessment centre will address the skills and knowledge required to fit in with the working style and culture of the organization. It is easy to say 'I get on with people', but at an assessment centre you can see how the person creates rapport with others and reacts to typical work situations. This is valuable information that far exceeds what the person can say. You are able to observe the candidate performing with other people and attempting to achieve goals, which will give greater reality to the words they have used.

Induction of new employees

Although it is rare that a candidate will match all the criteria that have been set by the organization, the results from the assessment centre will be able to show who best matches the criteria; they will also identify any gaps in their skills and behaviours. These gaps will form a proactive training and development plan for the new employee so that they will be able to settle into their new role more rapidly. This means that you never need to worry about not meeting all of the criteria, as all new employees need an induction into the new role, and by using the assessment centre process you will have a more measured and relevant induction that will help you to adjust to your new job. This is a positive outcome that can only come from a thorough assessment process. It helps both the company and the individual during those first few weeks of employment. By using the assessment centre approach, the organization will have an all-round view of how a candidate performs and fits the required role. This is valuable information that can only come from a practical approach.

What does this mean for me?

We have all come to expect that an interview will be a normal route to a job. This is still true with some companies, but as we have discovered above, too many are now looking at the assessment centre approach to enhance their decision making. It is likely that in the future the number of organizations using such an approach will increase even further, because they are now getting better recruitment outcomes. As this approach grows, you will be left behind if you are not aware of how an assessment centre works and how to perform to get the best result for you. You need to be aware of what may happen at such an event so that you can prepare effectively and – most importantly – show the real you to the organization.

You will not be the only person who wants your desired job; there will be others who will want it as much as or even more than you. Just telling an employer you really want the job will not get you ahead of other people. You have to do more than just persuade the employer that you want that specific job – you have to impress the employer with the skills and behaviour they are looking for in that role.

You may be tempted to 'wing it', if that has worked for you in the past. At an interview you can wing it to some extent, as it is just a series of answers to questions that relate to the job. However, your own experience will probably have shown you that the better-prepared people usually come out on top. The assessment centre has many different exercises where you will excel if you are well prepared. This will ensure you demonstrate your skills in the correct manner and show why you are a great candidate.

My experience of people who try to wing the process is that they tend to regret how they have performed at the end of the event. They know they could have done better but have recognized the facts too late. If you approach the day with confidence in your skills and have prepared as much as possible, it will come over to the employer who is seeing the real you.

It is all about options and preparation. If you do the work and prepare you will be ahead of the others in the process; if you fail to prepare you will come away with many thoughts about what you could or should have done. We will look at preparation and practice in future chapters. Ultimately, practice and preparation will really boost your confidence, and if you are confident about what you will face and how you will act, you are a large part of the way to success. You will be more likely to outshine your fellow candidates and be seen as a better fit for the job role.

Key points to remember

1   More employers are using the assessment process than in the past.

2   Employers want the best fit for their job.

3   Assessment centres are more reliable than interviews.

4   Failure has a cost to the organization.

5   This is a practical approach to see your skills and behaviour.

Reference

Dale, M (2005) *The Essential Guide to Recruitment,* Kogan Page

02
What employers are looking for

For a candidate, knowing what the potential employer is looking for is the most important information they require. If you know this information you can prepare effectively and slant your performance to stress the presence of these skills and behaviours, which could be the key to a successful job hunt. It may be difficult to find this information, but it is worth trying to identify what you can as it will give you a competitive advantage over the other candidates and boost your confidence in advance of the assessment process. This information can help with your decision making as well as your preparation for the assessment process. If you know what the employer is looking for, you can make an informed decision about which jobs to apply for and which to leave alone, saving your time and effort for the most relevant jobs.

To be able to find out what an employer is looking for, we must first of all establish how they identify the factors that are relevant to the job vacancy. Then we can identify how such factors may be tested at an assessment centre. Having done this, we are now in a good position to prepare positively for the assessment and offer ourselves as a credible candidate for the role.

As you can see in Figure 2.1, there are a number of key stages to the recruitment process. It can be time-consuming but following this process properly will ensure that the assessment centre is able to deliver exactly what the employer is looking for, leading to better appointments. Knowing this process is also key for the candidate, as it will give you a clearer view of the skills needed to not only get the job, but to succeed in it once you have it! We will look at each stage

Figure 2.1   The assessment process map

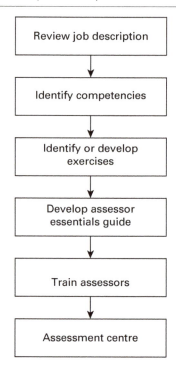

to identify what the organization is doing to prepare for the assessment process. We will then identify what actions you can take to gain a similar level of information prior to the event.

Review the job description

A job or role description is a list of the key tasks that make up the job. When a vacancy occurs, organizations first look at the job description to see if the role is relevant in the current circumstances – for example, can these key tasks be performed by current employees more effectively? Does the role need altering to reflect the current or future situation of the company? In other words, the organization will identify if the role is really necessary and in the correct form. Once these questions have been answered, the job description will be signed off as up to date and relevant for the recruitment process.

EXAMPLE JOB DESCRIPTION: Process leader

Lead the achievement of output, yield and quality targets for a large and complex work area and/or a larger crew of team members.

Responsibilities

1 Assume responsibility for a work area on a shift basis to deliver outputs against agreed production/time schedules, customer specifications and quality standards.

2 Ensure the availability of the resources required for production and maintain the optimum operating conditions for the plant and processes under their control.

3 Have an in-depth knowledge of work area processes, equipment and related instructions and procedures.

4 Ensure the proper set-up and daily routine checks of the work area are carried out.

5 Organize and instruct team members to complete work priorities and identify support requirements.

6 Identify and organize training requirements in the work area in line with process standards, paying particular attention to health and safety.

7 Respond appropriately to problems highlighted by team members and other work areas.

8 Ensure relevant process-related information is recorded.

9 Contribute to the development of the work area and performance improvement implementation.

10 Maintain a safe, clean and orderly work environment.

11 Contribute to the development and documentation of process standards and work instructions.

Skills and experience

Cumulative training and experience through the process ranks over at least a year is required to meet the full requirements of the role. Working knowledge of health and safety policy, procedures and legislation is essential; the process leader must know the quality standards expected and have the ability to train other operators to the appropriate level. Must be fully familiar with process-related documentation and recording systems.

Personal qualities

- Ability to work with others – works effectively with other team members; keeps other team members informed on issues affecting them; uses humour to reduce tension at work.
- Committed to achieving results – has the tenacity to get the job done whatever the constraints and difficulties encountered.
- Communication skills – has the ability to pass on information clearly and concisely with a range of people, whether spoken or written.
- Completer/finisher – starts and controls a process or procedure and checks that work has been completed to the appropriate standard in terms of quantity and quality.
- Concern for quality and customer – works in an orderly manner and recognizes the need for high-quality work and the need to meet agreed standards and priorities.
- Decisive in action taken – chooses the best solution from several alternatives to resolve a problem or achieve standards and priorities.
- Disciplined in approach to work – follows plans or schedules; completes work to deadlines and ensures that all steps and actions are followed; ensures proper shift handover is completed.
- Initiative – takes action on a problem or task without having to be told and identifies opportunities that will benefit the team or business.
- Leadership skills – takes responsibility for work area; co-ordinates the work of others; acts as a central point that others can refer to for help and guidance.
- Proactive in looking for better ways of doing work – welcomes and actively supports different ways of doing things; makes improvement proposals for his/her work area.

Once the key tasks have been agreed, the document will then be used to identify the skills the job holder must possess to be successful. The job skills may not be mentioned by name, but will be evident by the key tasks and what must be done to perform these tasks. For example, the job description may identify that the person has to deliver a daily brief to their team. You can identify that a key skill for this role will be effective communications and presentation skills. By reading the job description, it will become obvious what skills you need to have in order to succeed in the role.

It is worth remembering:

- Skills – these are talents and techniques you can apply to a given situation such as motivating people.

- Experience – this is what you have in effect done with your job, such as managed a project or recruited senior managers.

- Qualities – these are based on how you apply your skills to a given situation. You may motivate people but the quality you bring to this may be your tenacity as you do not give up on a situation.

- Behaviour – this is how you behave in a given situation. You may be able to solve problems but when doing so you involve people in the process. This is the behaviour that others will observe when watching you work, ie it is what you do.

- Achievements – this is what you have succeeded in doing in your role or in your social life. You will have various skills and behaviours that have led you to achieve the status of Director of Sales at an early stage of your career.

TRY THIS: Identify skills from a job description

Look at the example job description above. Read it carefully and try to think about what skills would be required to perform each task. It may be that more than one skill is required for some tasks, and some skills may apply to more than one task. Use the table below to list the tasks from the job description, and match each task to the skill or skills you will need for each task.

Table 2.1 Identifying skills

Tasks	Skills

How did you find that? I suspect you will have found some skills very obvious and easy to identify – but it might have taken a little more thought, and some real reflection of the tasks, in order to get some of the less obvious skills needed to successfully deliver on the task. When looking at the job description once you will get a lot of information. If you have time, it is worth reviewing this exercise again in a few days. You will find that you will add additional skills to the list as your subconscious has been working on the exercise.

It may also be worth looking at a job you have performed in the past and trying to identify the skills that it required. You are more familiar with the role and can dissect the skills more easily.

Now look at the model answer on page 210 in Appendix 1, where you will see some examples of the various skills for the role. This is not an exhaustive or definitive list – you might have thought of different ones – but it does give you a good idea of the range of skills to be thinking about for this example job. You will note that in my example I haven't qualified these skills with a level like high or intermediate, because from the job description alone it may not be possible to know what level of each skill the employer is expecting. You can establish the level of the skill by asking questions of the employer at the interview, or even over the phone prior to the event if you feel it is important. You will see that the skills clearly line up with the various tasks. By looking at these you are seeing exactly what an employer will identify. Therefore, we now have the required skills for a job.

The employer will be able to identify some key ways the skills will be employed. This will assist in identifying the different exercises that will be used in the assessment process. Knowing this, you can also do the same thing to a lesser extent. For example, the role may require regular communication with the team. The person in the role may need to use face-to-face meetings for briefing a group about their tasks, as well as walking the job and dealing with problems. Knowing that this is what the role requires, the employer will use this information to develop relevant exercises for the assessment centre.

And you can do the same thing. If you can identify the types of exercise you are likely to face, then you are in a good position to prepare yourself for the event. You will be able to practise these exercises and even research methods of effective delivery of the skill, which will add to your confidence prior to the event.

Don't forget that skills and competencies are different attributes. Skills are the accumulation of what you have learned in terms of knowledge and how it can apply to different situations. A competency is about how you apply your skill and knowledge to a task. We all know people who are good at a skill but fail to deliver good results because they either don't want to or are lazy. The competency is about the positive behaviours that are required to bring success to your endeavours.

Identifying competencies

Most organizations will have identified a set of behaviours that match the way they do business. These are called competencies and are clearly defined and understood by most employees. These competencies will be applied to a job role but they will not all be applied to every role in the organization. Each role will use the same competency framework but may apply a unique mix of competencies that apply to how that particular job operates. An example would be that a sales role may require influencing skills whereas an administration role may not.

Although we cannot know from the outside exactly what those competencies are, or exactly what this particular company means by each, you will find that most competency frameworks are actually very similar as they are attempting to define good behaviour in the workplace.

TYPICAL COMPETENCIES

Leadership	Tenacity
Teamwork	Flexibility
Problem analysis	Verbal communication
Problem solving	Written communication
Decision making	Planning and organizing
Influencing Interpersonal skills	Business acumen
Interpersonal skills	Continuous improvement
Creativity	

Let us look at the list of typical competencies. Again, this is not an exhaustive list but it covers most of the key areas that are common to most organizations. Most of these really are as self-explanatory as they seem – for example, leadership. Companies will have slight variations in their definitions, but however they choose to phrase it, we can be confident that the behaviour will entail leading a group of people to successfully complete a task correctly. Keeping this in mind, then, it is definitely worth looking at some typical examples to help you prepare for your assessment. The example here shows a multiple statement approach.

COMPETENCY DEFINITIONS

- Continuous improvement:
  - sets appropriate goals or standards for self, others and organization;
  - seeks to achieve appropriate standards or goals;
  - monitors progress regularly;
  - seeks to improve standards and methods of work.
- Problem solving:
  - seeks pertinent information;
  - recognizes what is important;
  - identifies real problem;
  - identifies causes of problem;
  - makes effective decisions;
  - commits to actions.
- Planning and organization:
  - establishes course of action for self and others to accomplish goals;
  - sets standards;
  - prioritizes workload.
- Leadership:
  - takes the initiative;
  - involves others in the process;
  - listens to views;

- motivates others;
- recognizes effort.
- Communication:
  - express ideas or facts clearly both in writing and orally;
  - considers the receiver;
  - listens to others' views;
  - responds in a positive manner;
  - communication is timely.
- Influencing:
  - acts persuasively and authoritatively to control the situation;
  - establishes effective working relationships;
  - works effectively in a team and involves others;
  - is adaptable/flexible in approach to situations;
  - understands opposing arguments.
- Analytical and data analysis:
  - evaluates data and courses of action;
  - shows a lack of bias;
  - reaches logical decisions;
  - understands the business needs.
- Teamwork:
  - works effectively with others;
  - shares ideas and listens to others;
  - prepared to work towards an agreed aim;
  - builds on others' ideas
  - does what is required.

TRY THIS: Which competencies will you need?

Have a look at the role you are pursuing and, from the list of competency definitions, try to identify the typical competencies that may apply. Be careful not to say that they all apply – although they may to a greater or lesser extent, the organization will be looking at the ones that have the greatest impact on the role and are essential for successful completion of tasks. Consider the key competencies that will help you achieve success in the role and record your answers in the table below.

Table 2.2   Which competencies apply to your job role?

1	6
2	7
3	8
4	9
5	10

This may not be an easy task to complete but it will help you think about what the employer is seeking from the candidates. By spending time looking at these competencies, you are becoming more familiar with what may be required. You are also getting into the heads of the assessors, as you know more about what they are looking for in the candidates on the day. You can consider how your skills match what is required.

Identify and develop exercises

From the work that the organization has completed to date we have a clear list of skills and competencies that are essential to the delivery of the job role. The list will have all the essential elements for success. Some organizations will try to prioritize the list into two categories. The first will be the skills and behaviours that will have the greatest impact on the success of the role, and the other will be attributes that will aid the success of the new employee but aren't absolutely essential for the successful candidate because such skills and behaviours can be learned as part of the induction programme into the new role.

This gives the organization a practical list to work with when deciding the next stage of the process.

The next stage that employers will take is to develop a framework to test the skills and behaviours of the candidates who want to be considered for the role, to ensure they test each area at least twice. This helps with the consistency of results. Each exercise will generally test more than one skill or competency – in this way, you can be delivering a number of competencies with each exercise.

Table 2.3 Examples of methods used to test competencies and skills

| Competency/Skills | METHOD | | | |
	Group exercise	Individual exercise	Role play	Test
Teamwork	✓		✓	✓
Problem solving	✓	✓	✓	✓
Interpersonal skills	✓		✓	
Tenacity	✓	✓	✓	
Verbal communication	✓	✓	✓	
Planning and organizing	✓	✓		✓
Numeric skills		✓		✓
Verbal reasoning		✓		✓

You will see (Table 2.3) that each competency or skill has a number of ways it can be tested. They are all interlinked in line with the way you perform a job at work; you utilize a mixture of skills and behaviours at the same time to achieve results. This should give you a good idea of the types of exercises you may come across at an assessment centre – in Chapters 5, 6 and 7 we will look more closely at how best to use this for your assessment preparation.

The exercises they will employ will be practical so that everyone can take part. If the event is for internal candidates only, they are more likely to develop their own exercises that match the internal data, culture and history. These will be exercises where the content may relate to the workplace and the department, and will draw on what is commonly known and shared within the organization. This will only happen if there is an expertise within the organization.

If the assessment centre has a mixture of internal and external candidates or only external candidates, the exercises will be more generic so that no one party has an advantage over the other candidates. Such exercises may have been used in the past or may be bought in from a consultant.

Should tests be used to look at skill levels, personality or aptitudes, these will almost certainly be bought in from an outside organization that has a product to match the specific requirements of the business and the role. These will be validated over many years and may have a score mechanism that can relate to the job type being recruited.

The organization will ensure it has enough material to fill the allotted time and that it offers the candidates an opportunity to demonstrate their ability against the competencies and skills required at least twice.

It is not unusual for an organization to try out the exercises to ensure they work well and achieve what they require. This can be done as a form of dummy run with different staff members, and will assist in removing any possible glitches in the materials.

The grid in Figure 2.2 demonstrates a real overview from an assessment centre that spanned three days. It shows all the exercises

Figure 2.2   Exercise and competencies grid

	Discussion	Simulation	Self-report	Presentation	Team exercises	Feedback	Select group	Role play	Feedback	Report	Presentation	Discussion	In tray	Group in tray	Review
Flexibility	×	×			×	×		×	×			×		×	
Business acumen	×	×	×	×			×			×	×	×	×	×	×
Teamwork	×	×			×		×					×		×	×
Leadership	×	×			×		×	×		×				×	×
Decision making	×	×	×	×	×	×		×	×	×	×	×	×	×	×
Problem analysis	×	×	×	×	×	×	×	×	×	×	×	×	×	×	×
Interpersonal skills	×	×		×	×	×	×	×	×		×	×		×	×
Planning and organizing	×	×	×	×	×	×	×		×	×	×	×	×	×	
Communication, written			×							×			×		×
Communication, verbal	×	×		×	×	×	×	×	×		×	×		×	×

that were used and the competencies they measured. You will see how some exercises appear to be repeated – for example, feedback is in there twice, but it actually has a different format each time. All organizations will have a grid like this, plotting the exercises against the competencies and skills. It acts as a checklist to ensure all competencies are covered at least twice (although, as in the feedback example, each repeated exercise will be measured in the same way against each competency, even if they are in a different format, to ensure consistency of results). The grid also ensures there is no duplication that is not absolutely necessary, and acts as a final checklist of contents.

What happens next?

The organization has a lot of work to do to ensure the assessment centre is a success. They need to develop the relevant exercises to test the skills and competencies required for the job. The grid will identify the types of exercises that are required; these will be a mixture of tests, group and individual exercises. These exercises will be developed and tested within the assessment team to ensure they deliver what is needed.

Each exercise will have an 'Assessor's Essentials' guide to illustrate what the assessor should be observing in a good candidate. This will usually have suggested actions that may be taken by a good candidate. Relevant score sheets for each exercise will also be developed. These two documents assist in the consistency of scoring and ensure the correct competencies are being observed in each exercise. This should ease the concerns of candidates who have not faced such a situation before.

Finally, the assessors will have a run-through of each exercise to ensure they are familiar with the content and what may happen. It will ensure the assessor is clear about what to observe and will complement the use of the assessor's guide and observation sheets for each exercise. This again assists in gaining a consistency of approach across all assessors.

My own experience with this process has shown that the assessors are proud of their role in the organization. They take the preparation very seriously and become familiar with the exercises and documentation. Most recognize that by doing the role in a responsible manner they are helping the organization grow and prosper.

Assessment centre

The final step is the assessment centre where the candidates get to experience the exercises and tests that have been developed. Like any interview, this is likely to be seen as an unusual situation by a candidate unfamiliar with the approach.

The observers want the day to go well and to find good candidates. They will be keen not to miss key actions from the candidates and keen to make a great final decision. They want the day to go to plan and for everyone involved to take an active part. The assessors will want all candidates to feel that they have been given a fair opportunity to display their skills and behaviours in a practical manner.

Then, at the final session (called a wash-up session) when the candidates have gone home, all candidates are discussed and compared against the skills and criteria for the role. Each person will be considered against the criteria and their performance will be given fair discussion. Often the problem might be deciding which of two or three candidates to appoint. This is a good position for the organization, as they have attracted a number of suitable candidates who can be considered able to fit the role.

I always found the wash-up session to be a good guide to how effective the whole process has been. If the level of debate and discussion is long and detailed, it is clear the assessors have taken their role seriously. I have never come across a wash-up session where the assessors wanted anything other than to ensure all the candidates were taken seriously and given equal time. This ensures consistency and transparent results.

As you can see, the process is quite rigorous, and has been developed over time to ensure the right result. There are no shortcuts because you are dealing with people's lives and work – it is essential for everyone involved to take their role seriously, follow the steps and use the helpful guides to come to a good decision.

When attending an assessment centre you will now know what has gone on behind the scenes to make the event work effectively. Most things that happen on the day are deliberate, so will form part of the decision-making process. Ensure you recognize that the steps that have been taken are for your benefit as well as that of the organization.

Key points to remember

1 A job description lists the tasks for a particular role.

2 The employer will use competencies as a way to define the behaviours required to fulfil the job role.

3 Exercises are designed to measure the skills and behaviours of the candidates.

4 Assessors/observers are trained to observe the competencies and skills in the exercises in a consistent manner.

5 Exercises will have an 'Assessor Essentials' guide to outline what to look for in each exercise and thus gain consistency.

How will it work?

All assessment centres will be different to each other, as the content will vary; you will never go through the same exact experience twice. This is because all jobs and organizations are different and have their own specific needs set against their culture and values. However, although the content will change, the process of each assessment centre will be similar, as ultimately, all organizations have the same desired outcomes – to get the best candidate for the role.

The process will usually be in six stages:

- invitation;
- start;
- exercises;
- interview;
- result;
- feedback.

TRY THIS: Expectations and concerns

Think about each of these stages. Try to identify what you will need to know about each stage – you can note your expectations and concerns in the table below. Consider your role as the candidate, and the role of the organization.

Table 3.1   Expectations and concerns

Stage	Expectations	Concerns
Invitation		
Start		
Exercises		
Interview		
Results		
Feedback		

Remember these – hopefully all of them will be addressed by the end of this book!

It may be useful to spend a few minutes considering how you will address any of your concerns with the assessment centre prior to the event. This will help you be even more confident when taking part in the process.

Invitation

You will receive an invitation from the employer, including the venue, date and time of the event. It may not explicitly state that it will be in the form of an assessment centre but one big clue is that you will be required for the full day – or even multiple days. Unlike a traditional interview, where the invitation will state the time and possibly the duration of the appointment, assessment centres will commence at the start of the day and will end at – for example – 4.30pm. Some invitations will clearly say what will happen on the day and may even ask you to bring a prepared piece of work such as a presentation. This is another clue that you need to be prepared for an assessment event. If you are in any doubt about it being an assessment event, you should contact the organization and ask what will happen on the day and how long you will be required. This will clear up any misgivings you may have.

Just like any other business appointment, it is advisable to contact the organization to let them know you will be attending. You can at that stage ask for any information that may help your preparation, such as the job description and competency framework. If you are unsure of the format of the day, you can ask at this stage. You may not get detailed answers about the exercises or tasks you will be set; however, you will know it is an assessment centre. This will assist your preparation.

The venue for the event may be at the organization's site, but this depends on the facilities they have available. It is not unusual for the venue to be either a local hotel or the organization's training centre, as such an event uses quite a lot of space.

The venue will be expensive if it is a hotel. As we have already seen, there are also more associated costs for the company such as the number of assessors and the time away from their real roles. This shows that the company is taking the process very seriously, due to the costs involved.

TOP TIPS: The invitation

Basic information covered by an invitation to an assessment centre event should include:

- date;
- time;
- venue;
- possible content;
- pre-work.

Start

When you arrive at the event, you will probably find there are a number of other candidates also attending. The number will vary but usually it will be between six and 10 people. You will be shown to either a waiting area or the main room that will be used for most of the exercises. This gives you an opportunity to meet others and find out about their expectations of the day. It is useful to mix with some of the other candidates as you are likely to be working with them on some of the exercises. It will also show the organization that you have social skills.

Most events will commence with the person running the process introducing those involved. They will name the assessors and maybe say something about why they are using this method to aid the selection process. They may talk a little about the role and offer details about the organization; this will help you establish if your preparation was correct.

The next stage is to give you an overview of what will happen during the event. This will outline the types of exercises you will face and give an idea of the timescales involved. The leader of the event will ask all candidates to give of their best in all exercises and try to be themselves throughout the period of the event. They may talk about the process of the day and what comes afterwards.

The outcome of the event will be described. This may be about how the person will be selected. It may also describe how training needs will be identified. The timescale of the next stage will be stated so that you will know when you will hear the result of the event.

As most events will have around six to 10 people, they can be accommodated in a main room and probably one other room, for individual interviews and splitting into teams. If you have a larger group, of course, there are likely to be more rooms so that the exercises can be carried out at the same time in manageable numbers. Where this is the case, you should seek out a plan or programme of the day which shows the whereabouts of the different rooms for each exercise, to reduce the chances of getting lost or confused.

However many rooms there are for the event, you can expect them to have enough space for you to work on individual exercises, as well as come together for group exercises with the other candidates. The room will generally be comfortable and laid out in a manner to make you feel at ease and able to work. Figure 3.1 is an example of how a typical assessment centre might set up the room; you can see that candidates are grouped together – not individually like in an exam setting – and that there's plenty of space for group work or exercises that involve moving about.

Figure 3.1 Typical room layout

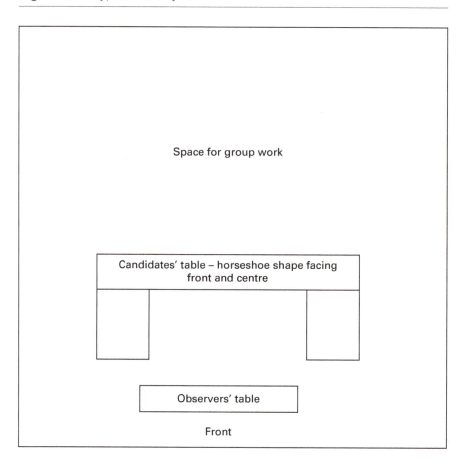

You will need to find a seat at the table that you feel most comfortable in. If given the opportunity, you can get to the room ahead of the other candidates so that you can select what suits you best, for example, if you will find it easier to hear or see nearer the front of the room. This is up to you though – there's no secret 'best spot'.

Around the room, there may be posters or banners depicting issues that matter to the host – especially if you are in the company's own training centre or headquarters. Be sure to look at these as they may help you identify key skills or knowledge about the employer. At a minimum it will demonstrate what is important to the employer.

From the employer's point of view they are trying to sell the organization to you. Even if you are not successful they want you to tell a positive story about your experiences. This enhances the employer's brand in the recruitment market.

Exercises

You will be required to take an active part in a number of exercises, most likely a mix of individual and group exercises. As we looked at in the previous chapter, these will relate to the skills and behaviours required by the organization to ensure the successful candidate meets or exceeds the requirements of the role.

Each exercise will be explained by someone from the organization using either a verbal brief or a written brief. It is important if you do not understand what you have to do that you ask at the time of the briefing. The assessors will most likely not be allowed to help you during the exercise, so don't expect them to input if you do not understand! If you receive a verbal brief for an exercise, make sure you take effective notes of the details of the exercise. If necessary, be prepared to repeat back to the briefer what you have understood as the key elements of the brief; you don't need to worry that repeating back the brief gives the others an advantage, as clarifying in this way shows that you know about communications and that a message must be understood to be effective. Most importantly, of course, it means that you will definitely understand the brief!

If you get a written brief for an exercise, the briefer will normally read this to the group. As the brief is being read out, underline the key aspects of the task; this ensures you have a full grasp of the key issues. Again, you can repeat back what you believe is important to ensure you have gained the correct information. We will look at these briefs and exercises in more detail in Chapters 5, 6 and 7.

The assessors will mainly be line managers from the hiring organization who have been trained to be assessors. It is a role they will only perform from time to time; most days, they will be doing their 'real' job as a manager at the hiring company. Other assessors may be drawn from the human resources department, and possibly some independent consultants will be involved. All of these people will want to see a successful assessment centre where they have obtained a good candidate for the role; they will see their role as having a positive impact on the process. They will have various rules they have to follow and tools they must use in order to be as impartial as possible.

All exercises will have a time limit to them as this will ensure all groups have had the same opportunity to complete the task in a similar time. You need to be clear of the allocated time from the start and work within the time limits during the exercise. Each centre will be different, of course, but it is most common that the assessors will only refer to time when the limit is reached. They will most likely not offer any elapsed time warnings, because the management of time belongs to you on an individual exercise and to the team on a group exercise. It's important, therefore, to make sure you are using the time beneficially – again, we will look at this in more detail in the chapters on specific types of exercise.

The assessors will be present during all exercises. They will try to be away from your direct eyeline and as unobtrusive as possible so as not to distract you from your task. They are likely to be in the corners of the room, not so far away that they can't hear the conversations clearly, but not so close as to confuse or distract the group. You may notice the assessors taking notes of what has happened and observing the group; in reality, each assessor will only be observing about two people during the exercise. They will note key issues and actions they have observed against a set of criteria for each individual exercise. In order to reduce interference or distraction, and give every candidate the best and fairest chance of doing well, the assessors will not interact with the candidates

There will be time between exercises and coffee-type breaks. You will not normally see the assessors at this time as they will be updating their notes. You can and should relax, but bear in mind that you are likely to be observed by someone from the organization, so it is best to stay positive and engaged as much as you can during the breaks. Spend time talking to the other candidates; it will show off your people skills.

You will see from Figure 3.2 that a typical programme will show you where you will be at different stages of the day. This will have been worked out in advance to ensure each person has completed each exercise by the end of the day. You will be able to see that the programme is developed to maximize the use of the day but also ensure you have suitable breaks to enable you to relax and eat.

Figure 3.2   Typical programme of events

Time	Candidate number									
	1	2	3	4	5	6	7	8	9	10
09.00	← Introduction →									
09.05 – 09.40	← Site visit →									
09.40 – 10.20	Ability test 1 →					← Shift report				
10.20 – 11.00	← Ability test 2 →					← Briefing →				
11.00 – 11.40	← Shift report →					← Ability test 1 →				
11.40 – 12.20	← Briefing →					← Ability test 2 →				
12.20 – 13.00	← Lunch →									
13.00 – 13.40	← Meeting →					← Meeting →				
13.40 – 14.20	← Teamwork →					← Teamwork →				
14.20 – 15.00	← Feedback →					← Interview →				
15.00 – 15.40	← Interview →					← Feedback →				
15.40 – 16.20	← In-tray exercise →									
End of day										

You will also observe a number of different types of exercise that are used for each person. This shows what type of exercise you will be involved with during the day as well as the order of delivery. You will note that everyone has the same programme but it may show that you complete the exercises at different times of the day.

You will get a series of exercises which will probably not seem to be linked. This does not matter; you need to show that you can adapt to the changes in the tasks and still be successful in delivering the correct results. Your flexibility will be noted.

The assessment centre is about all the exercises and how you work. There is never one exercise that stands on its own that must be completed successfully. It is your performance across the total exercises that counts. Therefore, if you feel you have failed in one exercise, move on and put it behind you. You can show other ways that you can be considered for the role.

TOP TIPS: Exercises

- Listen to the brief.
- Make good notes.

- Underline key tasks.
- Clarify what has to be achieved.
- Observe the time limit.
- Be flexible.
- Take an active part.

Interviews

Not all events have interviews. This is often a separate part of the process for some organizations. Where interviews are part of the process, they can be placed at different parts of the day.

There are two main methods employed with interview timing. One is to interview all candidates at the end of the event when all exercises are completed. This usually involves two interviewers per candidate, and so is manpower-heavy for the organization. Each pair of interviewers will see two or three candidates. The organization will not want you to wait too long for the interview as this is dead time. Often they will see first those candidates who have the furthest to go to return home.

The other method is to structure the interviews to take place during the day. Thus, two interviewers will see all of the candidates as part of the exercises. In such circumstances all candidates will have a separate programme that relates to them for the event. This will either be issued at the start of the event or will be displayed in a prominent place for all to see as and when necessary.

Results

Collating the results of an event is usually done by a 'wash-up' session involving all the assessors – the candidates will not be involved in this part of the event. The assessors will have observed different people during different exercises, and by the end of the event each observer will have observed all the candidates at least once. This allows each observer/assessor to make comments about all candidates. They will share their views about what they have observed and where each candidate fits against the organization's criteria. The usual method is to concentrate on one person at a time, so each person gets a fair discussion of how they have performed.

This can be a long and complicated process best done at the end of the event whilst ideas are still fresh. The result will be an agreement by the group about who if anyone should be appointed to the role. They will look at the training needs for those being appointed to ensure they can settle into the role effectively and efficiently.

Your results will be shared with you in either a letter or e-mail format. This will let you know if you have been successful or not. It is rare to get the result of an assessment centre on the day, and even rarer to get relevant feedback – more on this in a moment.

The letter or e-mail will let you know the next steps to take. This will involve accepting the job or seeking feedback if you were not successful. It is useful to seek feedback even when you are successful; it will give you a clear insight as to how you were seen during the event, and will help you when you first arrive and have a personal induction programme.

Feedback

All attendees will have the right to ask for feedback from the event. You will have given your time up to attend the event, so you need a professional level of feedback. This should outline what your perceived strengths are and the areas you need to improve. Such views are relevant to the organization and how it operates, but more importantly for you, will almost certainly help you with other job searches.

Make sure you ask for a detailed response from the organization to ensure it is useful to you in the future. To hear 'you were so close and all candidates were good' is of no use to you at all. This is far too general; you need to hear what you did well and its impact on the role. You also need to have explained where you were seen as not up to the required standard and what you could do to improve this area.

Always ask for specific examples of what you did or did not do. This will remind you of what happened and will help you see how to do better in the future.

The level of feedback you get will depend on the organization. Prepare in advance specific questions you want answered to address what you need to know to help you in the future. If the organization is reluctant to give feedback, send them a list of your questions for them to give a more considered answer.

POSSIBLE QUESTIONS TO ASK:

1 What did you see as my key strengths and where were they observed at the event?

2 What areas of my skills and behaviour do I need to develop?

3 How could these areas be improved?

4 What advice would you give me if I attended such an event again?

5 Can you advise me of other suitable employers you feel I should approach where my skills would be acceptable?

The way you ask for feedback is very important. I have experienced individuals who fight every comment and show all the signs of not listening. Such people will not get the detail they require as they will switch off the person giving feedback. Those who are friendly and listen carefully will get more detailed information that will assist them in the future. The person giving the feedback will want to feel they have helped rather than be in a battle. Always be polite and positive. It will ensure you are remembered if another role becomes available.

By asking these questions, you will be more aware of how your strengths and improvement areas were seen by another party. It may serve as a reality check but will enhance your own self-awareness when following other vacancies. When asking Question 1, you will get clear feedback about what you did well, which is reassuring and will aid you in future events as you will know to repeat what you have just done. Keep good notes as a reminder when you are next involved in a recruitment exercise.

The response to Questions 2 and 3 will give you a view not only of what to improve but also how to improve. It will show the employer that you care about your own development, and will demonstrate that you are open to feedback. You need to explore these two areas carefully and ensure that the person giving the feedback knows that you value what is being said. This will ensure the feedback you gain will be useful.

The responses to Question 4 will aid you in looking forward to a similar event and thinking about what to do differently. It is always better to be forearmed should you face a similar situation.

The answer to Question 5 may lead to a job prospect. Most companies have a network of suppliers and tend to know what is going on their own field of business. You will be surprised at the number of jobs that are not advertised; word of mouth is seen as a positive alternative to a long recruitment process. You can also ask if they would recommend you for a role if one existed with that other employer. This will demonstrate if they thought you were a good employment prospect, and a positive response will be a great boost to your confidence.

I have seen many a candidate recommended to another organization by assessors who have gained a good impression of the candidate and feel they will fit a role that they know of in another organization. This can save the other organization time and money in a search for a good candidate. By showing you are keen to work in similar roles, you open yourself to a network of other employers. For a more detailed look at how to effectively ask and prepare for useful feedback, turn to Chapter 11.

Practice makes perfect

We all need to see how these assessment centres work. The only way to become familiar with them is to attend as many as you can to gain experience. By becoming comfortable with the process and getting good feedback that you can act upon, you will start to improve upon your performance.

If you can get experience of these events before the main job you really want, you will be more confident when it really matters. This is not easy to do, but if you think far enough ahead, you can start to gain experience now.

If your organization uses the assessment centre process for recruitment, you can get experience of this by volunteering to be an assessor/observer. Most organizations struggle to get enough assessors, so you may be accepted more easily than you think. You will get appropriate training for the role, which will help you when you are taking part in an assessment process.

At the end of the event you will be tired due to the intensity of the day; all other serious candidates will feel the same. It is best to just get home and relax as you will not know the result for some time. Try not to socialize with other candidates afterwards, as this will only lead to a discussion on how each exercise went and what went wrong. You will feel worse for the discussion as it is not based on facts, only feelings. The other party may not care about the result as much as you and may cause you to feel bad about how you performed. Don't go there.

Key points to remember

1 Processes of assessment centres are similar.

2 The assessment centre will comprise a series of practical exercises.

3 All exercises have a time limit that you have to manage.

4 All exercises are observed by assessors.

5 You should seek feedback after the results are declared.

04
How to prepare for an assessment centre

With most things in life success comes only from hard work; it rarely comes easily to anyone. Most success is based upon solid preparation. An athlete, for example, will prepare with a detailed warm-up before a major event, so that they know their body is ready for the race. If they don't, they could pull a muscle and fail to complete the task as their body was not prepared to take part. In a more business-type setting, an effective manager knows that they need to prepare for major tasks – say, a key client pitch. Managers who try to bluff their way through any situation will fail to get the true potential from it; although they may have a natural gift for presenting, it requires proper preparation to see the pitch through to its successful conclusion.

Assessment centres are no different. Most people know that preparing for an interview is a good idea, and assessment centres too need good preparation in order to get the best result possible. You do not want to be in a situation where you fail to get the job and know it was down to not doing adequate or any preparation. This will provide you with plenty of reasons to kick yourself but will not change the situation.

You will probably think that you cannot prepare for what is a series of unknown exercises. On the face of it, you could be right, but there are some key things to do which will help with most situations, even if you don't know the specifics. If you merely turn up on the day and see what might happen you are leaving the result to chance; if you prepare correctly you are increasing your chances of success and boosting your confidence at the same time. We will look at how to make the most of the situation you will face and identify some actions you can take to maximize your chances of success. Follow these actions and you will almost certainly get better results.

There are five stages to good preparation for an assessment centre. These are easy to follow and have specific areas to pursue as best you can. You will need to take time out to prepare and use whatever resources you can gain access to in order to get the best result and boost your confidence.

The five key stages of preparation are:

1 invitation to the event;

2 arrival/geography;

3 practice;

4 advice;

5 advanced exercise.

Let us look at each of these in the order listed above. This is not a rigid order for preparation and you may well complete some of these stages at the same time; however, to ensure you get the maximum benefit from the approach, let's look at each separately.

Invitation

You will have applied for a job and will know something about the organization as part of the application process, but will probably have done little preparation prior to the notification that you were being considered for the role in the form of a formal invitation to the next stage. The invitation will give you the time and place of the event, and may also give indications about the format of the assessment. Most people will accept the letter as giving all the information you need to be able to turn up on the day and perform, but there is more you can do in order to be better informed.

You should contact the person at the organization who wrote the e-mail or letter to confirm your attendance on the day. Personally, I think it is better to talk to the person on the phone, as this way you will have made personal contact and will have an opportunity to make a great impression in advance of the event. However, whether you call or e-mail (don't write back by post, as you risk your letter being lost or turning up too late) you should definitely confirm attendance somehow. This is not only polite, as it will help the organization know how many people will definitely be attending the assessment centre, but you would be surprised how many people fail to confirm their attendance, or even fail to turn up on the day without notifying the organizers. Being diligent about your RSVP will show your politeness, organization and attention to detail before the day has even begun.

Now that the conversation is open, you can take the opportunity to ask for further information that will help you prepare. A note of caution on this – it can be tempting to use this contact to grill the organizer about any or all questions you have, but it's good to be aware of the impression you are giving while asking. Before you note down the information you want to request, check that you can't access it in other ways. Is the information in the letter? Is it available on the company website? You want to appear thoughtful and interested, not like you haven't paid attention! However, there are definitely things you can – even should – ask about. For example, if you do not have a job description for the role, now is the time to ask for one, as it will include more details about the role than an advert can accommodate. As we looked at in Chapter 2, it will also show some competencies that may be measured on the event. You can also ask about the types of exercises that may be used and any psychometric tests that will happen on the day; two other areas worth asking about are the company values (if these are not already available online) and the key competencies of the organization. They may be sent to you later, but this will be useful in your preparation.

You should definitely ask logistical questions that haven't been answered in your invitation, such as the dress code, the available parking or most convenient public transport stop, or if overnight accommodation is needed and provided. By asking these simple questions you will now know much more about what is expected on the day, which will be a big boost to your confidence before the event, and you will appear conscientious and engaged. Remember to be polite and thank the person you're speaking to for their help. You could say you are looking forward to the event and hope to say hello on the day – being friendly and polite leaves a good impression of how you do business with other people.

INFORMATION CHECKLIST

This is an overview of the kind of information you will want to know before an assessment centre. To make sure you have the answers, first look at the invitation, then do your own research, then you can ask any relevant questions:

- confirm attendance;
- job description;
- competency framework (if they have one);
- company values;
- dress code for the day;
- types of exercises being used;
- are selection tests being used? For example, psychometric/personality tests;
- car parking facilities/local transport;
- accommodation (if appropriate) for the night before.

Arrival/geography

As part of your preparation, you need to know how you will get to the venue in good time and not be late. Being late will create the wrong impression and taking chances with your arrival can only be regarded as risky; if you're not on time, the event may have started and you may miss some of the content, putting you at a distinct disadvantage to the others taking part. You should plan to arrive at least 30 minutes before the start. This gives you time to settle into your new environment and offers a buffer of time if something does go wrong. Don't worry if that feels too early to turn up – you don't need to go in until 15 minutes or so before the start, but that extra time leaves room for anything unexpected happening.

It can help to visit the site in advance if it is close to you, to establish familiarity with the layout of the building and correct entrances. Knowing this kind of thing in advance will boost your confidence. If you're planning to drive, you need to identify parking areas. The organization will probably offer this facility but you need to know how close it is to the entrance you require, and you don't want to be surprised by lack of adequate parking. If you are using public transport, you should become familiar with the routes being used and the timetable for the day. This will ensure your early arrival.

If the venue is outside your immediate living area, you can still become familiar with the area using an online tool like Google Maps. This will show where the venue is located and how to get there, and will give you most of the information you require to help you feel confident about finding the right place. You may also wish to consider an overnight stay in advance of the event; this will ensure better timekeeping and attendance on the day. Sometimes accommodation is supplied by the organization so this should be checked when you ring for more information. Be careful though – if you are staying in a hotel, don't rely on reception to give you a wake-up call. Ensure you use other means to wake up – such as the alarm on your mobile phone – to make sure you are not let down by other people.

Don't forget you are doing this to be better prepared for the event and also to feel more confident on the day, and it won't take long to check out the journey and venue, especially if you are local to the organization. It's often tempting to skip this step, but you should not be complacent, as it could cause you panic on the day – which could ultimately affect your performance.

Practice

At this stage you may or may not know what type of exercises you will be required to work on during the assessment centre. The invitation and the follow-up discussion may give you a lot of good information, and if that is the case you can look at how you may practise some exercises.

If you do not have this information you will have to look at the job description and advert; we looked at this in Chapter 2, but now let's cover it in more detail. Let us look at a typical advert for a job.

EXAMPLE JOB ADVERT

Team Leader required for the manufacturing department

The successful person will be required to manage a team of 10 people to achieve daily goals and work within defined budgets. They will report to the Manufacturing Manager, who must be kept up to date about daily progress against targets and people issues. The role will look at how to continuously improve the current output of the department. The Team Leader will work on maintaining harmony within the team and will be required to liaise with other departments to ensure you are giving the service required. Time may be spent on projects to enhance the total site productivity.

The job holder is an integral part of the manufacturing team and will be involved in site meetings as well as meetings with the department staff.

Just like the exercise in Chapter 2, we would now go through this advert to identify the skills and competencies required to succeed at this job as described. As we saw, there are different phrases and skills that you may get from it, but your list might look something like this:

1 Leadership skills – manage 10 people.

2 Interpersonal skills – maintain harmony and talk to other departments.

3 Communication skills – keep manager and workforce informed about targets and progress.

4 Time management skills – achieve targets and liaise with other departments.

5 Problem solving – achieve targets and deal with other departments.

6 Decision making – ensure smooth production.

7 Project management skills – work on site-based projects.

8 Meeting skills – meetings across site as well as in own department.

9 Teamwork – work with 10 people, other departments.

10 Budget skills – achieve output within budget.

Now – again, as seen in Chapter 2 – you will be able to identify typical methods of testing the skills and competencies of the role. That could look something like this:

1 Leadership – group exercises, possibly solving a problem as a group; may also test decision making and problem solving.

2 Interpersonal skills – group exercises and 'social' time.

3 Communication – a major part of all exercises, but possibly a specific report or presentation brief.

4 Time management – practical in-tray exercise (looking at priorities for the role).

5 Problem solving – group exercise, probably along with leadership.

6 Decision making – group exercise, probably along with leadership.

7 Project management – individual or group exercise with a relevant task.

8 Meeting skills – group discussion, maybe a mock project meeting, to also test project management.

9 Teamwork – all group exercises.

10 Budgeting – individual exercise creating or analysing data for a specific task or project.

As you can see, such a small advert offers a lot of detail about what is involved in the job and how it could be tested. The task now is to practise demonstrating these skills. We will look at some specific examples of exercises in later chapters so that you are aware of their structure and content; in addition, some of the exercises you may face may have answers on the internet. Take your time to look at these methods as this will enhance your confidence before the event.

A lot of organizations use psychometric or personality tests to help identify a good fit for the job role. We will look at these in Chapter 8, and again, you can also practise some psychometric tests on the internet. Other than practising your exercises, one area that you need to take time to prepare for is your knowledge of the organization, its products and the market it operates in. Such knowledge is often tested in interviews, reports and presentations. Without the prior research you will only have a vague idea about the issues, and too often individuals turn up for interviews knowing very little about the organization they say they want to join.

A friend of mine, when looking for their first job after college, interviewed for an IT job with a local council, and despite plenty of preparation about IT and its use in a working environment, was totally surprised to be asked what they thought a local council did and how each department was funded. These were questions that they had never considered when preparing for the interview. Needless to say, they could not answer any of the questions and made a very poor impression with the selection panel – and didn't get the job.

As you can see, neglecting to research the company as well as the job does not look good and can damage your confidence when you're asked even more questions – so don't skip this step!

Some questions that might be helpful to kick off your research:

1 Who is the parent company of this organization?
2 What are the main products or services of the site?
3 What problems do they currently face?
4 What difficulties have they faced in the past?
5 Who are their main competitors?
6 What advantages do the competitors hold over this organization?
7 What is the future of the market they operate in?
8 What new products and services are planned?
9 What financial and market information is available?
10 What are the main strengths of the organization?
11 What are the main threats faced by the organization?
12 Are there any potential changes to law that could affect the organization?

This may seem like a lot of research but in reality it is not; most of this information is available online. You will probably find many articles about the site or company, and you can get the financial information and annual report from the organization (marketing department) or from Companies House. This work will enable you to develop a number of relevant questions about the organization and will allow you to go into more depth about areas you find are relevant to the role. Candidates often worry about asking questions – asking too many, or too few, or the wrong ones – but this research will help you answer some of your potential questions before you get there, and will allow you to figure out what you actually want to know before deciding if the job and company are right for you. A good benchmark to aim for might be five key questions that relate to the future direction or markets of the organization as well as where your role will fit into these areas; not only will this help you understand more about the role, but most organizations will be impressed with a candidate that has researched the organization they want to join.

Advice

You may be nervous about the assessment process but this is a good thing as it shows you care about the job. Don't worry about the nerves as they are normal and most candidates will feel the same as you; anyone without nerves will probably not care how well they perform. You just need to be well prepared.

It's a good idea to seek advice from anyone you know who has experience of an assessment centre process: friends, parents, colleagues or neighbours. Never feel afraid to ask, as most people will be only too pleased to help. Ask about their experiences, and if they were negative, ask what they would do differently in the future. Ask them their top tips for feeling confident, and don't be afraid to probe further to really get as much information as you can. Again, many people will be keen to help someone who asks for it and appears willing to listen and learn.

However, do be aware that not everyone will offer correct advice or experience. I was running a series of assessment events for a client over three weekends at a local hotel. During the second event, one of the participants went missing at lunchtime, only reappearing about five minutes before we were due to restart, sporting a tracksuit and what looked like new training shoes. They asked if we should 'get on with it' and, to our surprise, dropped into a sprinter's position. When we asked what they meant, they replied that they were ready for the three-mile run and we should just get on with it – they'd been practising all week!

Of course, no such run was planned, and when we explained this and asked why the candidate had expected a run, it came out that a candidate on the previous event had decided to play a prank, and told them a run would be happening. They had advised that running kit would be a distinct advantage as the previous group had to run in ordinary clothes. As you can imagine, this was very embarrassing for the poor candidate! Although this is an unusual story, you should always consider the motives of people giving you advice, and only go to people you know you can trust.

Exercises set to be completed before the event

There may be occasions where an employer will set you an exercise that has to be completed prior to the event and brought along to the assessment centre. This is very important and needs to be given sufficient time in order that you do a good job. By giving you this in advance, the organization will be able to see how well you work on project-type issues without a tight timescale. Such exercises often have an element of research into the market or the company as well as looking at current issues. It is advisable that you do not leave this until the last minute – I promise, it always shows!

The nature of pre-work will usually be a report or a presentation. You need to ensure your work has both good content and a solid format; concentrate on both of these areas to ensure you do the best job possible. We will look at this in more detail later in the book.

It is useful to get other people's ideas about the content and also about the completed product. As with other advice, ensure the people you involve will tell you the truth about the output. Only constructive feedback will help; if the person tries to boost your confidence with false praise, they are doing you a disservice as it will hinder your progress rather than help. Ask them to tell you exactly what is good and why, as well as being honest about any areas they think you need to improve.

If you have a presentation to deliver, make sure you have plenty of time to practise the delivery. This will grow your confidence as well as make you more familiar with the content. Practise it a few times to ensure it flows effectively so that it will be perfect when you need it to be at the assessment event.

Finally, make sure you take the work with you to the assessment event. This may seem obvious, but I have known this work to be forgotten on the day on more than one occasion. It does not bode well and makes you look very unprofessional. In the worst instance it could make you late if you have to go back for it, which will dent your confidence just when you need it the most. It's a good idea to have a checklist of items to take to the assessment centre to help you perform effectively. This will include pen, paper, calculator (don't rely on your phone, as you may be asked to leave it safely with your things), pre-work and any other items you feel are relevant. By utilizing this checklist the night before and again before you leave for the event you can leave the house with confidence that you are fully prepared.

TYPICAL CHECKLIST FOR AN ASSESSMENT CENTRE

- Materials:
  - pen;
  - paper;
  - calculator;
  - letter or e-mail invitation.

- Pre-work:
  - report (printed);
  - presentation (printed);
  - memory stick with work on.

- Geography:
  - relevant tickets;
  - route map.

- Dress:
  - clean, smart, comfortable clothes;
  - clean, appropriate shoes.

Feel free to add anything to the checklist or remove items that are not relevant. The purpose of the checklist is to reduce your stress on the day and allow you to concentrate on the exercises you will face. It is worth considering now what else you feel you need to add to the checklist – for example, snacks, lunch if you have dietary needs, water, or any medicines you normally need during the day.

By following these steps to prepare you are improving your chance of success at the assessment event and building your own confidence by helping yourself feel in control of the situation. In most walks of life those who prepare tend to gain the success they deserve; by you preparing well you will get the success you deserve.

Key points to remember

1 Confirm your attendance at the assessment event.

2 Identify competencies and skills by reviewing the documents provided such as advert, job description, and values.

3 Complete any advance exercises early.

4 Get to know the organization and prepare any interview questions in advance.

5 Predict the exercises and practise for them in advance to boost confidence.

05

Individual exercises: communication

Whilst all assessment centres are different because of the needs of the organization, you can assume that you will be set various exercises that are either completed in groups or on your own. In this chapter we will look at working on your own on specific exercises concerning communication.

In this and the next three chapters you will see examples of exercises that I have used in various assessment centres. So, these exercises are real and may be similar to what you will face. I have explained what they are designed to achieve and how to get the best out of your performance on such exercises.

When working on your own you will be required to show your skills and behaviours that can relate to the job requirements of the organization. Most communication exercises will be in one of the following formats:

- written report;
- formal presentation;
- feedback to other candidates.

We will look at each of these exercises and review how best to approach them in a professional and effective manner. By doing this we are aiding our preparation and removing the mystery behind each exercise. For each one, we will look at what the assessors are looking for, one or two techniques that you could use to approach them, and one or two practical examples. For every type of exercise we will look at in this chapter and the following chapters, the most important thing is to always keep in mind the likely competencies that the assessors will be looking for from the exercise. They will be looking across a range of competencies – not just one – and will have an 'Essentials' guide which will outline what they expect to find in a good piece of work. They will look for these essentials in the work supplied by you; it's really important to consider what they might be, so you can include them.

Getting the brief

Most briefs you will receive will be in a written format that you will keep with you during the exercise. However, if you are briefed verbally, you need to be clear about what is expected of you in order to complete the task correctly. If it is a written brief, you should be able to underline the key actions you are expected to deliver. If it is a verbal brief, take clear notes of what was said and repeat the key areas back to the briefer. Be aware that an assessor may talk with a fast delivery. Whilst this will not be deliberate, you must be prepared to ask them to repeat what you don't understand or miss. If the delivery is slow, you need to concentrate on what is being said rather than fall for the natural tendency to think ahead. At all times you need to concentrate on what is being said. At the end of the brief, you should repeat what you believe to be the brief to ensure you have recorded the facts correctly. The assessor will probably see this as a positive approach, and, more importantly, it ensures you deliver what is required for the exercise.

For every exercise, you should always use the written brief, or the notes you have made, to check you have delivered what is required. Compare the original aim with your output towards the end of the exercise. This is the best piece of advice I have for all the exercises you may be offered in your assessment process.

Written report

When being set an exercise in report writing, we are being tested in more than just our writing skills. These skills are important, but there are other competencies that are being applied to this task, including influencing, problem analysis, decision making, planning and organizing, and business acumen. Therefore, you need to be able to demonstrate these competencies in the exercise, both in the content of the report and in how you explain your points. Typical assessor essentials for a report-type exercise will include:

- structure of the report is relevant to the topic;
- well-laid-out content for the reader;
- arguments are easy to follow, with relevant facts or details;
- easy to read;
- key points are made with examples or solid logic;
- key points are developed in the report;
- next steps or recommendations are clearly outlined;
- summary of actions matches the main body;
- demonstrates a clear understanding of the issues and what they mean for the organization.

We will all have different experiences of report writing and how to get our point across; whatever your experience level, you will need to focus on content and structure to ensure your report is effective. This may seem to take more time, but in essence you need to ensure you take time to plan the report before committing to writing, otherwise it is easy for your points to get lost. My experience shows that most people like to get started on the exercise and immediately start to write: this is usually a mistake. You need to focus on the reader and what they need to know. You should plan the main themes of the report and place them in a logical order.

When planning the report, you need to have a structure to the points you intend to make so that it is easy to follow. To be successful you need to plan the content that will be in each section of the report. Before you move to the structure, always ensure you have given the report a relevant title, showing what it is about. You should also date the document and ensure your name is indicated so the reader is aware of the relevance of the document both by timescale and by author.

There are two ways to complete the report: one is using a laptop and the other is writing it by hand. The organization will outline which is to be used, although some will offer the alternatives to you. Be prepared for each approach. If it is handwriting, ensure the assessor can read it. If your handwriting is very poor, use printing as an option. This looks better and is easier to read. If using a laptop, ensure the output can be easily transferred to the assessor either by e-mail or using a printer. You can ask this question prior to the event so you are prepared in advance.

Report layout

The layout you decide to use will depend on the intended content of the report. You have to select which format will best suit the brief and the reader's needs. After all, the report is intended for the reader, so they are therefore the most important individual in the process.

We need to look at a few layout options. These need to be clearly used to ensure the reader can follow the points being addressed. This will give you different options to utilize against the different exercises you may encounter.

Layout 1: Introduction, main points, and summary

This is the most basic report structure or layout. It is in three stages, outlined below:

- introduction;
- main points;
- summary.

This is the most useful structure for a report based mainly on facts and knowledge, which does not require either analysis or solutions to a problem or situation. This format is easy to follow and use, both as the writer and the reader.

Introduction. Here you need to state what the report is going to achieve and how it will be achieved. It can contain any back-up detail about your experience or knowledge of the topic that you feel is relevant and will enhance your standing. The introduction will only form about 10 per cent of the overall content, so delivering this section will require 10 per cent of the report delivery time.

Main points. These need to be clearly set out to support the issues you raise. They need to be in a logical order that clearly leads from one point to another. You will only need around four to six main points in most reports – too few, and you won't cover your content; too many, and you will overwhelm your reader or simply run out of time. Ensure you only include points that are relevant and logical, and keep checking your brief and title to ensure each point meets your needs. This should take up to 80 per cent of the overall content of the report.

Summary. This should include the key points of the report and act as a brief overview of the report's content. This section will need to be short and to the point. However, it also needs to be well considered as it will leave the assessor with a lasting impression of the report. You will want that impression to be positive and relevant to the requirements of the exercise.

Layout 2: C3PO

Another frequent type of report will involve looking at a situation or problem and having to offer your views and potential solutions. This is a more complex type of exercise that will need a different format than that shown above. You could adopt an approach to the problems-type exercise in an organization by using the C3PO format:

- current situation;
- problems faced;
- possible solutions;
- proposed actions to remove the identified problem;
- overview.

The above format is easy to follow as it has a clear logic to each section. It is often called the C3PO method after the famous Star Wars droid as a way to remember it. It is easy to remember and use as it ensures the reader has a clear logical argument to pursue in set stages. Let us look at these areas more closely.

Current situation. When you commence any type of report you need to guide the reader through the path you intend to take. In a simple report, we have called this the introduction, but for this approach we have called it the current situation. Here, you need to state what you will do and why it needs to be done. The 'why it needs to be done' will allow you to demonstrate your knowledge of the current situation with this issue faced either by the organization or in general. This will depend on the topic you are asked to report on. You can demonstrate your knowledge of what is happening so that it is clear in this first section that you are competent with the subject matter. By showing what you will do by the end of the report, you are gaining the attention of the reader and standing out from the other candidates.

Problem faced. This section of the report offers an opportunity to build on your grasp of the current situation, by going into the difficulties being encountered with the topic. It allows you to outline the key issues as you see them and explain in more detail any difficulties that may be encountered by the organization given your current level of knowledge. Unless otherwise guided by the brief (you may have been instructed to focus on one particular problem), a good rule of thumb is to try to identify at least three problems, as this will show a breadth of knowledge of the topic.

Possible solutions. This section allows you an opportunity to offer a range of practical solutions based on your experience. It is useful to outline the relevant pros and cons attached to each of your solutions. This will indicate that you know what you are talking about and have a number of relevant options that can be drawn upon. Again, a good rule of thumb is to outline at least three relevant solutions to show you can see a number of different approaches and demonstrate your broad thinking and your problem analysis.

Proposed actions. Here you are stating which option you believe best suits the situation. You need to build on your possible solutions and explain why your chosen solution is the best option to overcome the problems encountered. This allows you to show the key benefits and outline any potential threats to the solution. You need to show clear and logical thinking in this section to demonstrate that your solution can be workable and viable. It is a good demonstration of clear decision making.

Overview. Like the summary in the simple layout option above, this where you can summarize the key issues of the report. It should be a short section but can be important as it shows your ideas in a brief format and allows you to demonstrate your knowledge and analysis of the issues.

Preparation of a report

Now that you have chosen your layout, each area of the report needs to be planned so that you are aware of the content of each section prior to writing. This saves duplication of ideas. When planning what to put into each section of the report, we are best off looking at a horizontal plan concept of our points. This makes it easier to use as it is visual and flexible.

First, we need to identify the different sections of the report (see Figure 5.1). These are the headlines of each vertical line. Then we can list all the areas we will include in that section: you may want to consider using a brainstorm approach for each section, just to get all your ideas on paper – then you can narrow down which points to include by comparing them to the title of your report, and the brief, to make sure that each point is logical and relevant. (See Table 5.1.)

Our next step is to place the issues in order of importance to the reader. This is done by simply numbering each point under each section.

Figure 5.1 Horizontal plan for induction report

Introduction	Main points	Summary
What has happened?	Company History	
Why did it happen?	Department team	Programme of events
Who is responsible?	Department structure	
Purpose and Report	Department focus	Your views
	Your role	
	Relevant history	

Table 5.1   C3PO horizontal plan for company problems report

Current	Problem faced	Possible solution	Proposed action	Overview
Existed 10 years	Lack new ideas	School visits	University twin	Difficult times Need positive
Current products	Market slowdown	Diverse Internal University twin	Diverse approach	approach
What is working	Diverse base	Do nothing		
	High competition for staff	Outsource work		

It may look a bit messy but it saves time trying to rewrite or reorder the points. You can see this demonstrated in Figure 5.2 and Table 5.2, where the numbers against each item show the order of delivery. This saves rewriting the list as time is better served writing the report.

As you can see, it is quick and easy to plan and order your content. If you have a different method that works for you, that's great, but whatever method you use, it is essential to plan if you want to have a clear and easy-to-read structure to your report that makes your points relevant in a logical manner within a strict timescale.

Figure 5.2   Completed horizontal plan for induction report

Table 5.2   Completed C3PO horizontal plan for company problems report

Current	Problem faced	Possible solution	Proposed action	Overview
Existed 10 years (1)	Lack new ideas (3)	School visits (4)	University twin (2)	Difficult times
Current products (2)	Market slowdown	Diverse internal (3)	Diverse approach (1)	Need positive approach
What is working (3)	Diverse base (2)	University twin (2)		
	High competition for staff (1)	Do nothing (1)		
		Outsource work		

Delivering your report

In all cases, use the first five to 10 minutes of your time to plan what you will write. You could use the horizontal planner to ensure you can easily order your thoughts and ideas, and when the plan is complete, re-read it to ensure you have not missed any key points. Re-read the brief to ensure you have completed all that was requested. It may seem obvious, but too many candidates fail exercises because they cover what they wanted to, instead of covering what was requested.

Some further basic principles when writing reports:

- Remember to title and date your report, and put your name at the start of the paper.

- Title and number your sections to aid the reader, eg 1. Introduction. You could also include other visual clues such as indenting the first line of each new paragraph, bullet pointing key points, or using line spacing between sections.

- Ensure you complete the report inside the timescale – include the time you have in your planning.

- Re-read the brief to ensure you are familiar with what is required before you take a last look at the report. You now have the time to re-read the content of the report and correct any mistakes. This will ensure you have achieved what you set out to do and thus satisfy the assessor and the needs of the exercise.

Reports are a good way to demonstrate your communication skills and show the depth of your current knowledge. By carrying out and using a solid structure your points will be well documented by the approach you employ. This approach will present you as a good candidate for the role.

Practical examples

Let us look at some typical exercises you may face during a typical assessment event. These are real examples and can be applied to most organizations and situations you may encounter. When reading the examples, try to think about what structure you would employ and what content you could develop to fulfil the brief.

EXAMPLE BRIEF: Written report
Your induction

We want you to consider what sort of induction you feel will be necessary should you join the organization. Consider the timescales for the issues you want to include. You have 30 minutes to complete a report on your induction. You should complete the report in no more than 1,000 words. This can be completed either by handwriting on paper or using your laptop.
Good luck.

This is a simple report based on your thoughts about how you can quickly fit in with the organization. You will need to share your current knowledge of the organization as well as details about what you don't know. Because this is mostly delivering simple facts and opinions, you would probably be best advised to use the introduction, main points and summary approach for this exercise.

You will be able to show your business acumen and self-awareness as well as your skills in planning and organizing. This will show that you have some of the required skills for the new role. Your written communication skills will be on show as you deliver a great report. By using the horizontal plan techniques, you will be able to quickly plan the content and order of the report. Taking time to do this will make the writing process easier and will add to the flow of the report.

There are no real catches in this exercise as the content is about you and what you feel you require. Feel free to be as open and honest as you want with your content; you can use the time to outline some of your strengths that will demonstrate how you will settle into the role quickly and effectively, as well as show your self-awareness and problem solving by recommending induction activities that you would realistically need in order to succeed. To really take this a step further, you also need to show a practical side by outlining not just what you feel needs to be done but also why it is necessary and the potential benefits to the organization.

The 1,000 words is usually a guide – it works out to approximately two and a half sides of typed A4 paper. Whilst you will not be tested on the exact number of words, you need to be close to the word count. If the report is too long, it will disengage the reader and will not represent you in a good light. If it is far too short, it will appear that you have very little to say or that your self-analysis is lacking. It could also indicate that you did not plan and organize the time you had available, so you did a rushed job. This will not show off your skills.

If you want to see what such a report could look like, there is an example answer on page 211 in Appendix 2. I'm sure it goes without saying, but this example report is only good because it is specific to the individual who wrote it, and the particular role they were applying for – it won't be anywhere near as effective if copied for someone else's use! It can, however, act as an example of layout and the type and depth of content assessors will probably be looking for from a brief like this.

EXAMPLE BRIEF: Written report
Organization problems

Over the past two years the organization has gone through major changes to the way it operates, some due to legislation and some to the current market situation.

You will need to write a report of no more than 1,500 words and present this to your assessor in 40 minutes' time. The report will need to outline your thoughts about how the organization can further develop in the next two years to ensure it remains competitive in the current market.

Good luck.

This is a more complex report as it requires you to have researched the organization and the sector prior to the assessment centre. Internal candidates will seem to have an advantage as they have worked through the problems. However, your view as an outsider can offer a different perspective on the problems so don't be put off by the task. You are not at a disadvantage over internal candidates as it is known by the assessors that some people have insider knowledge. The assessor is looking at your analysis of the situation as you see it; there will be no right answer. They will be looking at your analysis, problem solving and decision making.

In this example you would be better off using the C3PO approach to address the brief correctly, as it allows you to demonstrate your knowledge and offer practical solutions. It will clearly show your ability to analyse a problem in an organized manner – this is almost always more important than insider knowledge of the company. For an example answer, please turn to page 215 for Appendix 3.

TRY THIS: Written report practice brief

You should now try to apply the content of this section by writing a report about what induction you feel you would require in order to fully settle into a new organization – you can use the brief from the first example on page 60. When you have completed the report, you can compare it to the example answer on page 211, or better yet, give it to someone who will offer you constructive feedback that will help you write even better reports in the future.

TOP TIPS: Written reports

1 Ensure you have clearly understood the brief.

2 Allocate your time between preparation and writing.

3 Use an appropriate format for the content.

4 Re-read your final product when you have finished.

5 Use headings and indent the content to aid the reader.

Formal presentation

Most assessment centres have an element of a formal presentation in the format; it is an easy way for assessors to identify a number of key competencies in their candidates. These will most likely include verbal communication, business acumen, interpersonal skills, planning and organizing, decision making and problem analysis – or some combination of these, depending on the brief.

A lot of people dislike delivering presentations and will dread this aspect of the assessment process. If this is you, know that you're definitely not alone in your apprehension; however, try to look on the presentation as an opportunity, not a threat. Presenting can be a great chance to show your skills and confidence to an assessor whilst making a number of good points about your knowledge – and by carefully planning and practising, there is a lot you can do to offset nerves!

Let's look at what typical essentials an assessor will look for when you deliver a presentation.

Delivery:

- delivered the presentation with confidence;
- kept good eye contact with the audience;
- points made in a clear and concise manner;
- checked message was understood;
- used appropriate visual aids.

Content:

- introduced self and topic;
- outlined what will happen during the presentation and why;
- shared the main issues logically;
- shared any areas of concern;
- stressed positive actions or remedies;
- summarized the key points;
- asked for appropriate questions at the end;
- gave clear and precise answers to any questions;
- thanked the audience at the end.

Presentation layouts and planning

There are two main types of presentation that can be requested. These can be summarized as:

- presenting facts about a known issue;
- developing a new idea or solving a known problem.

Just as with written reports, for formal presentations you will need to consider the structure of your presentation. Having a clear structure which supports the type of brief you have been given will be crucial to keep the focus of the audience. You can use the report structures from the previous section to address the two types of presentations. For presenting known facts or simple opinions, you can use the simple introduction, main points and summary approach; the C3PO approach is more suited to a presentation about delivering a solution.

You can prepare for the presentation using the horizontal planner. If you have both a report and presentation to complete, the horizontal plan can be applied to both exercises. The planner is easy to use and will ensure that you include all the issues you feel are relevant, in the correct order. Your content will be both logical and comprehensive. It is just as important to prepare for a presentation as for any other exercise. You need to spend time at the start being clear what you want to achieve. You should then plan the format of the delivery. This can take time out of your resource allocation but it will save you effort later on as the presentation will be easy to follow and will match the brief you were asked to address. Unlike a report, for a presentation you will always build in some time to practise your delivery. By having one or two run-throughs you will be able to identify any necessary changes; it will also boost your confidence when delivering in front of the assessors. You will be able to ensure you are able to fill the allocated time effectively and not run over the time limit.

Delivering your presentation

As can be seen from the assessor essentials list, delivery is just as important as content for a presentation. There are a few concrete ways in which you can try to look and sound confident both in the presentation and with the answers to the questions, showing that you believe in the content and boosting your credibility with the assessors.

First, spending time on your planning will ensure you remember to outline what you will do and how long it will take, meaning your audience will clearly understand what you're trying to communicate. You can also use your planning time to think of a good 'hook'; a way to get attention by stating a fact or some other interesting point. A good hook will set your session apart from others, helping your presentation to stick in the minds of the audience.

Another tip is to be honest in your presentation, as the questions will show up any areas where your experience is light. It can be very tempting to try to bluff through areas where you know less or feel less confident; however, this will almost always show up in any detailed questions. Instead, where you feel you do not have the experience in a particular area of the job, be open about it, but outline how you feel it can be remedied. Offer a practical way to enhance your skill or knowledge of that area as this will show your analysis but also willingness to learn. After all, everyone has to learn new skills and knowledge during their career. You can even give an example of how you have applied yourself to such an area before and share the success you had as a result of your positive application.

When faced with questions, be clear you know what was asked. If you are unsure, paraphrase what you think the question was or ask the panel to repeat it. There is no point in answering the wrong question as it will not represent your communication skills as well as you would like. You do not have to have instant answers to any questions. If necessary, you can give yourself time to think and develop a clear answer. Always be positive in your answers and make reference to past success in any related areas. This shows that you have applied yourself in the past and will be more than willing to do so again.

All of this will help you to feel confident; to help you look confident, you can use confident body language such as open gestures and keeping eye contact with the panel or person who asked the question. Avoid folding your arms; this looks defensive. Don't be tempted to put your hands in your pockets; this makes you look unsure or too casual.

A presentation can also share some features with an interview, in that you may be offered the chance to ask questions of the assessor or panel. If this happens, focus on the areas you have tried to express as needing development. Ask how the panel feel about developing the skills you require or how they feel such skills will be acquired.

Try to be positive about any presentations you have to deliver. They can be stressful, but with clear, structured planning and rehearsal, a well-written and well-delivered presentation will show you as a confident person who has key skills to offer the organization.

Practical examples

Let us look at some examples of presentations you may be required to complete. As with the reports, when you look at these examples, consider which structural approach and planning system you might use.

EXAMPLE BRIEF: Presenting known facts

You need to prepare to deliver a presentation in 30 minutes' time. This will be delivered to a team of three people and will last for 10 minutes. You need to look at your career to date and highlight aspects in which you have great pride and offer examples of aspects you feel you need to improve. You also need to identify which parts of the job you have applied for best suit your skills and which parts would require further development.

After the presentation you will be asked relevant questions by the panel of three.

Good luck.

This brief looks fairly straightforward at first reading. However, you need to note that there are two parts to the exercise. The first part is reflecting on your history and the second part is looking forward to the new role. Whilst these need to be addressed separately, you need to consider more about how closely you fit the new role and spend more of the presentation time on the future than on the past. Any assessor will want to know about the past, but their major concern is about the current role to be filled. They will know more about the current role as it is their organization. They will know little about your past and the organizations you have been involved in.

If you are not familiar with presentations, there is a template structure and format in Appendix 4 on page 219; you can use this to cover all the aspects of the presentation. You just need to fill in the gaps so that the presentation flows. It is a quick method of preparing a presentation ready for delivery.

EXAMPLE BRIEF: Presenting knowledge of a subject

You are required to deliver a 10-minute presentation to a panel of two people in 40 minutes' time. The presentation needs to focus on how you see the current situation regarding Brexit and what steps our organization needs to consider in order to succeed post-Brexit.

Good luck.

This is a typical presentation about your knowledge of a subject and how you can apply that knowledge to a real situation. It could easily be about the current market affecting an organization or how a marketing campaign could be used to develop the organization. This exercise requires you to show your relevant knowledge of the topic and then demonstrate how it will be used in the real situation the organization may face. Therefore, the presentation has two main areas: the current situation and what can be done in the future.

Note that in this brief there is no mention of questions at the end. Don't be fooled – this will almost certainly happen anyway. Be prepared for a series of questions about your logic and approach; even if you do not get any questions it is of no concern as you were at least prepared.

Your time needs to be balanced between these three areas. Where you know little about the details of the organization, feel free to give various alternatives and explain why each has its own merits. This will demonstrate that you have a broad approach to the topic. Try to avoid only having one idea, as it may not be favoured by the group; try to show a broad approach. When answering any questions after the presentation you can describe in detail why you thought different ideas would work. You can show how the ideas are governed by the circumstances and that you would need to know more about the organization's circumstances. It is a good idea to identify how you would gain such knowledge to help formulate a solution.

TRY THIS: Presentation practice brief

Prepare and deliver a presentation about your key skills and what skills you feel you need to be even better at your current role. The presentation should last for 10 minutes. Deliver the end result to a person who will offer effective feedback. You can let them use the presentation format as a guide for what you need to include in the presentation.

TOP TIPS: Formal presentations

1 Be clear what you have to do.
2 Plan your time between preparation and delivery.
3 Use the appropriate planning and delivery format.
4 Ensure you sound confident by modulating your voice.
5 Face the audience and smile whilst using open gestures.

Combined brief

It is also common that there is a combination of a written report that has to be presented back in the form of a formal presentation. This may be given as two separate exercises, as we have looked at already in this chapter, or a joint brief may be used.

How it works

The assessor essentials used to outline what a good candidate will do will be the same for each of the two exercises as they are for the individual exercises. The main difference will be that you will be expected to manage your time effectively over two large tasks. This may seem difficult at first, but it is the same as when completing individual tasks: you need to be clear about what you are doing in the exercise. A good technique, as with all of the exercises, is to spend a few minutes planning what you need to do to make an effective impact on the exercise. This should include a time plan for each part of the exercise to ensure you are able to complete both tasks to the required level. You can also use the preparation tools utilized in the individual exercises above, as well as the various delivery tools such as C3PO.

When you commence the delivery of the exercise, you need to be aware of how you are using the time available; check how you are utilizing your time against the plan you developed at the start. A good rule of thumb is to check your progress roughly every 10 minutes – this is enough time to have made some progress, and still allows you time to re-plan if you have gone off course. This will ensure you deliver what is required within the timescale. Always plan to have a little time at the end to review what you have completed, check it meets the requirements, and if necessary, make any small adjustments.

If the two briefs are given separately, ie one after the other is completed, be aware that the report may be taken away at the end of the first part, so ensure you keep any notes you have taken as preparation, to assist your memory when preparing the presentation.

EXAMPLE BRIEF: Combined brief

You have been offered a potential grant of £1 million to fund the implementation of your business idea.

You have 90 minutes to prepare your business case in the form of a written report and a short presentation in order to finalize the grant and be able to launch your business.

You will be required to present this in a maximum of five minutes to a panel of your peers, followed by questions and feedback.

You are at liberty to structure the report as you see fit; there are no constraints other than the time available.

TOP TIPS: Combined brief

1 Plan what you have to achieve.

2 Plan your time across the two tasks.

3 Use the planning tools for each exercise.

4 Utilize the delivery tools for each exercise.

5 Regularly check your progress against the time limit.

Feedback to other candidates

Offering feedback is an area of the job most people tend to dislike. We can often equate feedback with criticism, meaning that we feel uncomfortable giving or receiving it – it can feel rude, or awkward, or undermining. In reality, feedback is absolutely vital as a method of helping you – or the person you are feeding back to – to do better at what you do. It should act as a motivator to the receiver to aid their development, and is a great tool to have at your disposal if you use it correctly. However, in reality we have all probably suffered from some form of negative feedback in our lives as it is usually so memorable. The intention may have been to help us improve, but the delivery probably made us feel worse. There are many resources out there to help you learn how to give really helpful and constructive feedback and avoid this negative consequence, but particularly in an assessment centre, we do need to lose our natural reluctance to give feedback if this forms part of the process. We need to start to feel positively towards the exercise and how we can offer someone a motivational discussion.

In an assessment centre setting, the feedback session will be either at the end of a group exercise such as a problem-solving discussion, or at the end of the event as a whole. The more normal approach is to be told in advance that the feedback will be required at the end of the exercise. At times it may be thrust upon you with little notice, though this is rare. The organization will use this type of exercise to test for decision making, interpersonal skills, verbal communication and problem analysis.

The Assessor Essentials will be used to identify if you can deliver feedback effectively. Assessors will probably be looking for you to:

- set the scene at the start;
- identify the key issues;
- analyse the key issues;
- create a rapport with the other person;
- involve the person in the discussion;
- seek the other person's view on key points;
- give praise where it is due;
- consider the impact on the individual;
- create a positive atmosphere throughout;
- correctly identify what needs to be achieved;
- develop an agreed way forward;
- thank the person at the end.

Verbal feedback methods and approach

Feedback is easier if you think of it as a two-way process. If you do all the talking in the feedback session, you will be unable to establish if the other person is engaged or agrees with your points. When you use a two-way approach, you will be able to check understanding and hear the other person's views – which may even support your views. Having a true two-way conversation will also help you to avoid the temptation to be too nice to the other person and leave out areas of feedback that you feel they may disagree with or take offence at. It's important not to fall into this trap, as it will make you look like a person who avoids the issues or – worse still – who cannot see them in the first place.

Another pitfall to avoid is to think that the obvious things you have seen do not need to be mentioned. For example, the person you are giving feedback to may have done a great job otherwise but missed one key area. Even if you think everyone knows that they missed this area, and it's easier to focus on the overall good performance, it is your role to both give praise for the good performance and help them by identifying what could make them even better. This is not picking at small items, as you are giving a balance to the process. It's about being objective about your feedback – and demonstrating that you have noticed what needs to be noticed.

The balance with feedback is so important. If you paint too black a picture you are likely to face resistance. You need to get the balance between good performance and improvement in the correct proportions. You will generally find most people warrant 70–80 per cent good performance; therefore, that balance should be replicated in the feedback. It's a good idea to start with the good items to show that you have seen all the good work; starting with constructive praise can help with establishing that two-way conversation and rapport. Then you should move onto the improvement areas. This will show you can see what is important and also motivate the person receiving the feedback to make the necessary improvements. Any feedback that is too negative will usually be rejected by the receiver. They will not like what they are hearing and will want the process to stop as quickly as possible. This will not end in a positive result. The key, then, is not only balance, but to ensure that both positive and negative feedback is specific and constructive – it should be helpful, not vague or discouraging.

Constructive feedback method 1: Open-ended questions

In order to ensure your feedback is specific and constructive, it helps to have a 'layout' or structure you can use, just like with the reports and presentations. The simplest structure is to open with a question, for example, 'How do you think that went?' From this, you will know before you start talking if they agree with your thoughts or not. You can then offer your views in a way that responds to their impression of their performance. Your views should then stimulate a discussion. Remember, you are leading the conversation – keep any discussion forward-focused on what the person can do next time. You cannot change the past, but you can develop in the future. In this way you can develop an action plan to go forward.

Another simple method is to ask, 'What do you think you did well and what needs to improve?' This is slightly more leading, and you may find that the answer to this focuses on what needs to improve. Even though it is the other person taking the lead here, you still don't want the conversation to focus too much on what went wrong, so it is best to take control and insist on talking about what went well first, before you look at the improvements. Note that I have used the word improvements rather than what went badly – this is deliberate, and a trick you can use. It's a more positive word which gets a better response because when talking about improvements as opposed to dissecting mistakes, it is easier for the conversation to focus on developing an action plan for the future.

Constructive feedback method 2: POOSA model

Another method for giving feedback is the POOSA approach. This is a slightly more structured way to get a positive response and create a two-way dialogue, and is a great method if you feel less confident with allowing open-ended questions to structure the discussion. It operates as follows:

- positive impact;
- observed improvements;
- opinion (receiver's);
- solution;
- action plan.

In order to be effective, the POOSA process needs to be introduced to the person as a way to put them at ease. You should outline what you will do and how it will be achieved. Stress that it is a two-way process and ask the person to input whenever they feel the need.

Positive impact. The process starts when you give feedback on the positive things you observed. Ensure you give a lot of examples and relevant detail – even praise is unhelpful unless you explain why the good thing is good. Try and get an acknowledgement of the content from the other person before you move onto the next stage.

Observed improvements. You can then give your views on what you observed that needed to improve and why. This needs to be fact based, not really your opinions of the work – keeping to the facts helps to keep the conversation dispassionate and constructive, whereas if you are too opinion based, it is more likely that it could feel awkward or confrontational.

Opinion. You have done most of the talking at the start. It is now the turn of the other party; you need to ask their opinion of what they did and of your views. Encourage them to say what they agreed with, and also what they disagreed with. This will turn into a discussion about facts – again, remember to keep this discussion solutions-focused. You don't want a debate about who is right.

Solution. The person then needs to be encouraged to develop solutions to the improvement areas. If they are really struggling, you could offer suggestions, but be wary of coming across too dictatorial here – only they can commit to the future actions, so it's best that the ideas come from them if possible.

Action plan. Once the solutions are agreed, you can both develop an action plan for future improvement. This will need to outline specific actions and timescales. This is a positive end as it is forward-focused and should be practical.

For a scripted example of how a verbal feedback conversation might follow the POOSA model, please see Appendix 5 on page 221. As you can see from the example there, the feedback is fairly easy if you get the involvement of the other person. You can deliver your feedback with confidence. Always keep relevant and detailed notes for giving feedback. A good tip is to use a tick to indicate positive actions and a cross against improvement areas against your noted points. This makes it easier to summarize the two areas when giving feedback.

Difficulties with feedback

Feedback exercises are the only individual exercises in an assessment centre setting which share some of the drawbacks of group exercises – namely, that you will have a certain level of reliance on the other person. Let's look at some ways you can remain in control of your own performance even when dealing with someone unpredictable.

Remember the observer is looking at your skills in delivering the feedback. You need to show that you involve the other person and can see the positives and improvements in their performance. The structure you use will depend on the person you are dealing with. If you get little input from the other person – short or vague answers – you will need to outline your views and ask for a response. As long as you stay calm and have relevant and accurate details to feed back, you will appear to be doing a good job. If the other person disagrees or has little to say, you need to manage this in a positive manner. Remember, they will not be doing their cause any favours if they are deliberately being obstructive! If this happens, don't panic; just remind yourself that it is your role to help them, but if they do not want help, you cannot make them change. Changing the person is not your goal here; your goal is demonstrating that you can give fair, constructive, helpful feedback. Remind yourself of this and think of your goal while you are suggesting practical improvements.

You can sometimes come across a person who has failed to make an impact on an exercise or has not performed well. This can be difficult to handle as you will not want to be too critical of another candidate. Again, the key to this is to remember your goal in this situation – it is your role to give feedback, not to give compliments! You simply need to consider the other person's feelings and ego, and give your feedback in a clear, thoughtful way. Don't be tempted to skip the difficult conversation; if you fail to identify the key areas of improvement, it is you who will be seen by the observer to be lacking in skill, so you need to develop an approach that will allow you to keep control and develop improvement in the individual.

For situations where you are concerned about someone's poor performance, and are worried that they may take the feedback badly, a slightly modified version of the open-ended questions model can be used. Start with the same sort of question – for example, 'How do you feel you performed in that exercise?' – which should get a response that you can work with later. If they identify it was a poor performance or that they did not contribute, then great – you don't need to break the bad news! You can then move the conversation on by asking what they would do differently if the exercise was re-run, and from this you can develop an action plan that is practical and relevant to the individual.

If they cannot identify any way to improve, or if they don't see that they need to improve at all, it becomes harder to manage the conversation. However, you can still use your open-ended questions technique. For example, you can talk about a specific moment in their performance and ask what they would change about it. You can focus on the impact of their actions (for example, that the person who had a query seemed to leave the conversation feeling discouraged and unhappy) and ask if they had noticed it. You can do this a few times, and this should hopefully encourage the person to engage with the conversation and offer some input, which then gives you something to work with to develop an action plan.

Feedback may seem a difficult area to tackle as it is rarely part of your day-to-day role. If you are seen as being good at this you will tick many boxes for the assessor. You will be seen to be a good communicator and have great interpersonal skills when dealing with others. You will be seen as a person who is able to observe and analyse a situation and not miss what is happening.

Practical examples

Let us look at typical briefs you can get when feedback is required in an assessment centre.

EXAMPLE BRIEF: Presentation feedback

You are about to hear a series of presentations from your colleagues. Each of these will last 10 minutes. When all the presentations are completed you will be selected to give feedback to one of the presenters. The feedback session should last no more than five minutes.

This at first seems very straightforward: you have to give feedback that will last five minutes. However, at this stage, you do not know who you will be offering feedback to. This makes your task a bit more complicated, but not difficult. You simply need to keep notes on all candidates, as you will not know who you will deliver your feedback to until after the presentations.

Usually, after the presentations you will be told who your feedback will be delivered to and in what order. You will be given a short time to prepare your content, say five minutes. Sometimes the feedback will be in front of the total group one at a time. In other cases you will be paired with someone who will also give you feedback. In all cases you will be observed.

If it is one-to-one feedback in pairs, try not to be too friendly and miss any of the key points. You have to do a good job. Sometimes the other person can be brutal in their feedback to you, but don't be tempted to get your own back. Remain professional and use the POOSA model. The brutal approach may be because the person has no idea how to give feedback. This will be noted by the observer, as will your response. Be as positive as you can and remain professional.

If you have the total group giving feedback one after the other, it is tempting to offer to go first and get it over with, but it is best to let someone else go first so you can see what is happening with the total process. You can use the extra time while the first feedback is being delivered to prepare your session so that it is even better.

Be mindful that some observers are aware of this and will ask a group member to offer feedback to the person who has just given feedback. This keeps the group's attention and prevents you getting extra time. Therefore, only do the extra preparation after the first level of feedback has been completed. Also, keep some notes of the first delivered feedback in case you are selected to give feedback on that.

EXAMPLE FEEDBACK BRIEF: Role play feedback

You have just been observing one of your colleagues in a role play of a work situation. They were dealing with one of their team who had a query. You have five minutes to prepare a feedback session to help this person should they face the same situation again.

In this instance, you have not been told in advance what would happen – that you would be giving feedback – and so have little time to prepare. If you have taken notes it will help you a great deal. If you haven't, take a minute to make some as soon as you receive the brief; in this example, you would need to think about what moved the conversation forward and what held it back.

Because of the relative lack of preparation time, with exercises like this one, the open-ended question technique will likely serve you more effectively than the POOSA model. You can start the feedback by asking the person, 'How do you feel that last session went?' and offer your views on what was said in the practical situation. Then you can ask the person, 'How would you have acted differently if the person came back in the room now?' These questions will guide you through the feedback as you can input after each of the answers to the questions. It is a two-way approach, which takes the pressure off you as a candidate to have all the answers, because you should be responding to what your partner is saying. It's still a good idea to use the final point from the POOSA model wherever you can though; ideally, all formal feedback exercises should end with an action plan which will represent what has been discussed.

TRY THIS: Giving feedback practice brief

You need to practise giving feedback in order for it to flow more easily in the assessment process. You should prepare to deliver feedback to one of the following people:

1 a person who has just cooked you a meal;

2 a friend who has just talked about a news item;

3 a recent sports incident you either took part in or attended;

4 a person who has given you a lift in their car.

It's a good idea to get your chosen person's agreement first! Deliver the feedback and then ask them to feed back to you on how it went and what could make it even better.

TOP TIPS: Giving feedback

1 Keep notes of what the other participants have done well and what they need to improve.

2 Make the feedback two-way.

3 Use the POOSA model to offer feedback.

4 Always end with an action plan to improve.

5 Offer relevant praise as well as improvements.

Key points to remember

1 Always be clear what you are expected to achieve.

2 Plan what you intend to deliver.

3 Plan your time against the tasks to be achieved.

4 Use a clear structure to your delivery to aid the assessor.

5 Check at the end that you have delivered what you planned.

06
Individual exercises: analysis

Whilst all exercises have a communication element, there are some that are specifically designed to see how you analyse data and make effective decisions. These exercises allow you to demonstrate specific skills that will be required in the working environment you will face if successfully recruited. These exercises are designed to identify how you work when analysis of information is required. There are many forms of this type of exercise, but they can be broadly summarized into these five areas:

- in-tray prioritization;
- business case study;
- self-evaluation;
- role play;
- rating other candidates.

We will examine each of these five types of exercise and suggest methods to employ to demonstrate your skills and behaviour at its best. As with the previous chapter, you need to be clear about the objective of your brief and what you are expected to deliver in the allocated timescale. Always check you have delivered what is required by reviewing the brief at the end.

The in-tray priority exercise

These are exercises where you have to apply a priority to a series of work activities. It is used to see if you can demonstrate judgement, decision making, business focus and time management.

The assessor essentials for such an exercise will usually include:

- exercise completed within the timescale;
- all parts of the exercise are completed;
- identified the main priority ratings;
- identified the low-priority items;
- identified items for suitable delegation;
- actions were designed to keep the organization moving forward;
- can apply business acumen to the tasks;
- has clearly identified the key result areas of the role;
- planned and organized the workload effectively;
- has a method for prioritization.

These exercises usually look daunting at first. They may comprise, in their simplest form, a list of 20 actions that require prioritization. In a more complex form it may be a pack of 30 e-mails with different activities and sometimes more than one activity in each e-mail. However complex or simple the task, the main thing an employer is looking at is whether you can see what is important and what is not important to the role, with the items provided in the exercise; you can see that most of the assessor essentials are related to this main skill.

Approaching an in-tray: grid method

There are many models and methods available to help you prioritize, and maybe you already have one that works for you. My preferred method is the speed/impact grid. Set up a simple grid on a piece of paper. The two axes are the importance of the task (measured by the impact on the business of the task and its outcome) and the deadline (or speed of delivery). By placing each item or task on this simple grid, you can clearly see which to prioritize; tasks that fall towards the top right of the grid are needed very soon and have an important impact on the business, so should be highly prioritized. Tasks that fall towards the bottom left are not needed soon and will not have much of an impact, so should not be prioritized. In the example grid shown in Figure 6.1, you can see that item 3 is clearly more important than item 7, because it requires speed of action as well as having greater impact on the business.

Figure 6.1 Priority grid

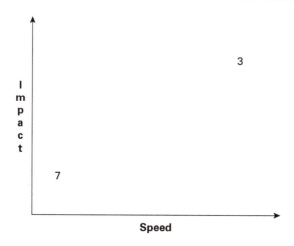

This is a simple way to help you prioritize items with a clear process that demonstrates you know what you are doing. Once you have the tasks in order of priority, you now need to say what action you would take. This should be relevant to the priority, and should also show you understand how an organization works. People will look at this grid and will be able to identify the following actions from each quadrant.

- top right – do now;
- top left – do later today;
- bottom left – delegate to someone;
- bottom right – this does not need to be done by you at the moment but can be passed on to someone else.

Practical examples

Let us now look at what you may face in various exercises. We will look at the brief you will receive and identify what you need to achieve.

EXAMPLE BRIEF: Simple in-tray

You have just been asked to stand in for a colleague who will be missing from work for six months. You cannot contact the person and know little about the issues they face. However, you know the role is responsible for 10 production operatives and you have to maximize the production output. You need at least nine people on the line at all times.

The role is a Team Leader and you report to the Production Manager. Your new manager is off-site until tomorrow and cannot be contacted. You are about to go on holiday, which cannot be cancelled.

You have to deal with the workload you have found on your desk. You have 40 minutes to complete the task. You need to identify the priority order of each of the 20 items and must say what action you would take with each item.

Good luck.

Workload tasks

1 The sales manager wants you to attend a meeting in three months' time so they can show you a number of potential new products and get your ideas.

2 The line need to know the workload for the shift today.

3 Your manager wants some ideas to improve productivity on the line by next week.

4 A director wants you to order some envelopes from the stores.

Let's unpack this example. If you highlight or underline the key areas of the brief you have to work on, you will identify what has to be done in the exercise – in this case, two things. First, prioritize the various items and then say what action you will take on each. To help prioritize in any of these tasks you need to identify how the role operates or is judged by the assessor.

You will note that this role is judged by the identified key result areas of maximizing production and managing 10 production operatives. Therefore, you need to prioritize around these two key areas. Items outside this area are irrelevant or add little value to the performance of the role. This gives you a way to prioritize that can be applied to most situations.

Look at the four tasks in the example. As we know, the key result areas are to maximize output and manage 10 people, so the first step is to try to put these four items in order of priority, and then identify what action to take for each. For both key result areas, it is clear that the second task has to be your priority – your team will need to be briefed on the day's workload so that production can run effectively, or they won't be able to achieve any output at all that day.

The least important from this example is task 4. It may be from a director, but it is not specific. There are details missing, such as what size of envelope and how many are needed, as well as the date required, so your only action is to offer a simple e-mail asking these questions and stating who will deal with the query in your absence (remember, you will be on holiday soon!). Too many people deal with this first, as it is a request from a director and this makes them feel it must be important, but in this example, your role is to set business priorities, not keep people happy.

Tasks 1 and 3 also have little immediate impact on your key result areas. You cannot offer ideas for task 3, as you know nothing about the issues – you are too new in this scenario to have had the time to learn. However, there is a shorter deadline given, meaning that *something* is required, as you're unlikely to be back from holiday in time to deal with this. An e-mail response would be appropriate, explaining that you are on holiday and have just arrived in the role. In our example scenario, the requesting manager will know this, but a response like this shows that you have understood the importance and haven't simply ignored the request – plus it is polite. Task 1 is probably the third on the list; you have no date for the meeting but you are likely to be back for it, and the subject is important as it will impact your line. Again, an e-mail confirming you would like to attend and asking for the date would suffice.

Note that in this example, we have not only prioritized and chosen an action, but there is clear reasoning behind each. In this kind of task, it is important to not only say what you would do, but also to explain why you would approach it that way. This will ensure the person reviewing the exercise understands your thought process. For example, you may have chosen to put tasks 1 and 3 the other way around if you were doing this task, and as long as you have clear reasoning and a logical justification for your decision, you can still show that you understand why you are taking certain actions, which is the kind of thinking and skill the assessors are looking for.

EXAMPLE BRIEF: Multi-stage prioritization

This is a diary of a shift from a company that manufactures paper products. This is a blow-by-blow account of the shift. You need to summarize this diary and present it in a written form for the next shift. You need to outline any actions you feel are necessary.

The shift is the 7am–2pm shift. At the start of the shift there were two people short on the crew. The two people who have not come to work (A Jones and B Davis) have not made contact. The lack of two people caused only a small problem with running the plant.

One of the other areas was able to supply one person, so the start-up of the machines was delayed by only around 10 minutes. Later in the shift, B Davis rang in sick and is probably not going to be back on shift for at least five days. A Jones has not made any contact at all.

A call was received from M Amis on Crew 1. He has flu and will probably not be on his next two shifts. He was concerned about passing on the flu to his colleagues.

During the shift, problems were experienced with the toilets. There is no soap in the workroom and the toilet paper is running low. The cleaners have also failed to clean the manager's office again.

At around 9.00am there was a problem with the stacking on the machine. We put it right in about 15 minutes. This was done by blowing out the offending pieces of paper from the jaws of the machine.

Martin Smith has noticed that the guard on the stacker has come loose. It is not a major problem as the machinery still runs.

A reel change was needed at around 12.00. This took around 45 minutes. This was longer than usual because we could not get a fitter for 15 minutes. We maybe should have run the machine until the fitter arrived. Once the job was started it was completed quickly.

The canteen was busy today. There were long queues for breakfast. To help make up for this, half the crew were allowed to take a 15-minute break during the reel change. The rest for the same break later in the shift.

At 10.00am we noticed the reel diameter was 40 mm too large. This caused some problems.

The fire alarm check took place at 9.30am. It seemed to go well. The crews were unsure if it was a real alarm and did not know what to do. They were told at the time it was only a test. Some did not believe it.

The product was not of the usual quality. We could not decide what had caused this. After a discussion, the problem seemed to rectify itself. This has happened before. We rejected 10 minutes' worth of production.

At the end of the shift the product cut problem reappeared.

During the shift three people reported for first aid for cut fingers caused by the slitters. These were all dealt with without any lost time.

The machine efficiencies were as detailed in Table 6.1.

Table 6.1   Efficiencies table for shift diary example

				PREVIOUS SHIFT	
	Budget	**Actual**	**Rejects**	**Actual**	**Rejects**
M/c 1	89%	89%	3%	89%	3%
M/c 2	75%	70%	20%	75%	1%
M/c 3	90%	85%	13%	86%	10%

At a briefing today by Sales we were brought up to date with future orders. It is expected that we will gain a lot of new orders in the next two weeks. These will be for immediate delivery. This will mean that we need to increase our efficiencies and reduce our rejects. If we fail to fulfil these orders we may lose some of our current workload.

You have 40 minutes to complete this task.

This example is another form of priority exercise you may face, where you are asked to read a piece of work and then decide what is important to pass on to the next person via a report. It will usually involve an overview of a number of tasks and will require several steps in response. As you can see, you will get more time to respond to this kind of exercise.

As you can see, there are two parts to this brief: you are first required to summarize the issues that have occurred on the shift in the form of a log, and then you need to identify any relevant actions for the next shift coming into work. This example looks at a production-type role but a similar exercise can be used for any role in an organization. The key is that even though you're not given a list of tasks like in the first example, this is still a prioritization task and should be approached in the same way.

First, we must summarize the diary. Instead of deciding what to do first, the priority decision here comes from deciding what is important for the next shift to know. As you will see, there are a number of non-value issues that do not need to be in the shift log, such as the reel change and the canteen as well as the cleaners/toilets. These are non-value-added items as they are not part of the role and are for information only. The reel change is part of the role but has been completed.

Just like the reports and presentations we looked at in Chapter 5, the shift log should be clearly structured, so it's worth taking a couple of minutes to plan. In this example, the log could be delivered using headings to highlight the key points for the next shift. My headings might be:

- Labour availability/staff absence.
- Machine efficiencies.
- Product quality.
- Safety.

Once the shift log is complete, the next part of the task will be more familiar, and you will be able to use the log to identify things that the next shift needs to do. In this example, these might be:

- A review of machine efficiencies for machines 2 and 3 – we can tell from the table that reviews are done every shift (because previous shift numbers are indicated). We can also see that machines 2 and 3 had higher levels of rejects, and the 'actual' number is lower than the 'budget' number. Even if we have very little idea of what these numbers actually mean, we can still tell that actual is lower than budget, and that readings seem to be taken every shift – so it's a safe bet that the next shift will need to do this.
- An information briefing for the workers on the next shift, covering:
  - the actions to take in the event of a fire alarm;
  - to be aware of cuts being caused on slitters;
  - the procedure to ring in if ill in the future to help plan labour needs;
  - that there have been some problems with the cut on the product.

Finally, once you have identified the tasks, you can apply the grid method to prioritize them. There's a lot here, but this exercise can be done in 40 minutes if you plan carefully by creating a set of relevant headings to address the main issues. These headings will save time and maximize your understanding of the issues, and your approach will demonstrate to the assessor that you see an overall picture, not just a set of unconnected points.

Challenges and variations with in-tray tasks

When facing any kind of prioritizing exercise, as we have seen, you need to have a logic for your decisions and a process for your answers. Be careful to identify these at the start as it will present you as a good candidate and will allow you the time to complete the exercise correctly. However, there will almost always be two or three items that cause an internal dispute. If this happens to you, don't panic, and don't get hung up on choosing the 'correct' order – it is much more important to get them into an order with some logic. By using the grid method – or other simple time management techniques – to identify the priorities of the role, even if you end up with a different order to the order the assessor expected, you will be able to show your clear decision making and the logic behind your answers, which is really what they're looking for.

Similarly, if you don't manage to complete the whole exercise, it is not a major problem as long as you have identified the main key issues and can show your logic and decision making clearly. Therefore, always work on the most important items first, as this shows that you can prioritize a workload. Try to avoid the natural tendency to do the easy items first, simply so you feel you are making progress; if time runs out, the assessor cannot see what the key items are, as you have only worked on the trivia. This will not represent your ability or knowledge in a positive light.

An additional variable of this type of exercise is the potential for it to be turned into a group exercise at the end. When everyone has completed the task or time is up, you may well be asked to discuss and agree the priorities of the work you have just completed. Again, don't panic as this is a typical group exercise. It will not happen every time but you'll be ready for it if it does. We will look at how to handle group exercises like this in Chapter 7.

Whatever task you are given, there are a few tips that will help you face any challenge or variation of this type of exercise:

- Take your time to read the total brief. It is not unusual to find that tasks are linked, or cancel each other out.

- Make notes or comments (on the paper if you are given a printed written brief) that will help you recall the key facts. This can help prevent re-reading of the items and hence save you time.

- Sometimes you will be given several pages – basically, paper versions of each task. If you are, you can put these in physical order as you go about the task to help yourself keep track.

Practice: in-tray prioritization

Let us look at a larger exercise to help you focus on a number of issues. Remember to first read the brief carefully, underlining or highlighting the key parts. Use the grid method to help you prioritize, and make notes that justify your decisions.

TRY THIS: Priority

You are running a customer service department responsible for answering queries that have been raised on the telephone. Your customers expect answers within 48 hours.

Today is Monday 1st May and you have just returned from a two-week holiday. The time is 9.00am and you have to go to a customer service conference at 11.00am. This will last the rest of the week, and you cannot cancel your attendance.

On returning to work you have found a number of issues on your e-mail which must be addressed. You have to prioritize the issues and say what you would do with each item. You have a team of four people, all of whom are very busy on Mondays. Your manager is not available until Wednesday 3rd May.

Items to address

1   A customer, Mrs Rose on 0191 222 3333, wants you to ring her regarding a query concerning a rude employee.

2   You are invited to a meeting in the training department at 9.30am on Monday 1st May to discuss your team's training plans.

3   The Director of Finance wants an estimate of your team's overtime for the next three months. This requires you to discuss your team's workloads with them. The estimate is required by Friday 5th May.

4   You need a cartridge for your department printer as you are onto the last one from stock.

5   There have been a number of complaints from customers regarding the delays in answering the phone. The Customer Service Manager wants to know what action you intend to take.

6   You have been nominated to be part of project team to look at widening our customer bases. The team members must report their action plan for the project to the Chief Executive by Monday 8th May. The Personnel Manager is the Project Team Leader.

7   A new trainee will be arriving in your department at 9.30am on Monday 1st May. You have this person for three months.

8   One staff member, Dave Orf, wants a day's holiday on Tuesday 9th May.

9   One staff member, Ivor Complaint, has asked to see you about a grievance.

10   A staff training session needs to be planned for the next two weeks.

11   You are invited to a briefing session at 10.30am with all managers. The session will outline the plans for the organization and will be taken by a director.

12   One staff member was off ill last week and may not return to work today.

13   Your ideas for improving the company image are required by Wednesday 3rd May. All managers' views are needed. Supply to the Human Resource Director.

14   The company conference is to be held on 3rd October. All managers are requested to recommend a theme for the event and a potential venue. Whoever suggests the chosen theme and venue will be on the top table at the event. Your ideas are required by Monday, 8th May at 10.00am.

15   Your telephone is ringing and one of your staff is indicating that it is a difficult customer; they are asking you to handle the call.

16   Your post is in the mail room and cannot be delivered as the mail room staff are short-handed.

17 Next week, Tuesday 9th May, the company will launch a new product; you need to make sure yourself and your staff are familiar with the details as you may get inquiries.

18 Your staff want to have a social evening next week.

19 You need to check your pension details to ensure they are up to date.

20 Your manager is on holiday in two weeks' time, so you need to check if there are any tasks he wants you to do in his absence.

Table 6.2   Priorities

Priority	Item no	Action	Reasons for the action
1			
2			
3			
4			
5			
6			
7			
8			
9			
10			
11			
12			
13			
14			
15			
16			
17			
18			
19			
20			

How did you find this exercise? For an example of how this task might have been completed, see the model answer in Appendix 6 on page 224.

TOP TIPS: In-tray prioritization

1 Read the total brief before you start.

2 Start with the important areas first.

3 Use the grid to evaluate each item.

4 Explain what you will do and why.

5 Identify suitable headings for a shift log.

Business case study

This is an area that may be used by organizations to try to simulate a real work-type situation. Most organizations tend to use bought-in exercises that have worked in various types of organizations in the past. These exercises are tried and tested and usually have a correct answer. They will usually be used to assess verbal or written communication, business acumen, problem analysis, problem solving, decision making and data analysis. The typical assessor essentials will be:

- ability to analyse the data;
- develops reasoned arguments backed up with facts;
- establishes priorities;
- offers reasoned solutions that match the problem;
- communicates ideas coherently;
- can offer reasoned arguments;
- completes the exercise in total and on time.

Types of business case exercise: methods and approach

These exercises will vary in nature and it is difficult to predict if they will be used as part of the process. They are not used as much as the others described in the book, but you do need to be aware of them. They will generally take longer to deliver and may have a number of aspects to the solution.

Read, report and present

The most common type is an exercise in a booklet format. This booklet will contain details of an organization or situation, requiring you to spend time to really understand all the factors you will need to consider. Typical of this type of exercise will be a series of stories about an organization that needs to go through a major change. Each department will have a history and an outline of the key staff; there will be financial tables as well as output data. You will be asked to analyse the situation and determine what you believe should happen next.

When dealing with this type of exercise it is best to take your time reading the information provided. Make notes on the paper to help you remember the key facts and save time re-reading the script; you will have plenty of time to do this, as it is not unusual to be given three hours for such a task. The outputs will usually be a report of your findings or a presentation with questions, and sometimes you will be required to deliver both. As with every exercise, you need to be totally clear about exactly what is required from you right from the start, and plan your response by allocating time to each task to ensure you conform to the time limits. Refer back to Chapter 5 for specific advice on reports and presentations – those models and techniques will apply in this kind of business case exercise as well.

Whilst there may be a certain answer the assessors will consider correct, try not to worry about 'passing'. Just like in the other types of exercise, showing that you have applied a clear logic and decision-making process is usually more important. You can still offer different alternatives and describe which you prefer and why, which will show you have considered other options and have the capacity to look at issues in a broad sense. It will show that you understand that one answer is not always the right approach. Be prepared to explain your thinking, and always be positive about why you believe something is right.

Data-driven business simulation

Another type of exercise takes the form of a business simulation, and is more likely to be computer based. You will usually get some advance information to read or access to online data to help you prepare in advance for the exercise, which for this type will usually be about change in an organization or financial data. You need to be clear what the exercise is supposed to do to be able to develop the answers. On the day, you will be given total access to the remaining data. You will usually have to make decisions at different stages of, say, a three-hour period. After each decision, you will get feedback on your answers. This allows time to prepare for the next stage. Always consider the feedback and take your time with your answer – unless you are specifically asked to, there's no need to be drawn into a fast response.

People issues

A final type of simulation may involve people issues, and may revolve around a disciplinary case or a grievance. Such exercises are generally shorter in duration – usually around 30 minutes to an hour. They almost always involve a degree of pre-reading about the person or the situation.

In this type of business case, you will be given records of the individuals, as well as the relevant policies and procedures. Just like with the other types, make sure you read all the data and make relevant notes on the copy provided. You will then be asked to make different decisions about what to do at regular time intervals. After each time interval you will be given feedback and will be required to make another decision.

Take whatever time you have to make each decision. Consider the impact of your action on the person and their colleagues. Also ensure you are following the agreed policies and procedures at all times.

How to approach a business case study

It is difficult to prepare for business case studies as they vary so much; however, you will notice that they share common features with the other types of exercise we've covered in these chapters. As with everything you are asked to do at an assessment centre, the most important thing is to take your time to really understand the brief and be confident of what is expected of you. It is important to act positively and not make too many assumptions; if in doubt about an action, consider any potential problems that may arise and look at how to overcome them as part of your decision.

You may be given a multiple-choice approach to the actions. If so, look at each option very carefully and do not exclude any of the answers until you have given them due consideration. Again, take your time with each choice as it will impact on what you have to do next time around. You will get no credit for giving quick answers if there is plenty of time available for the analysis.

If the case study is about change, don't start looking to implement the answer immediately. You always need to have a plan that has the input of the key people involved. The plan needs to be communicated and accepted by the organization; only then can you start with the pilot for change and an evaluation. Finally, you can place the full implementation of the solution into place. Try to follow a logical approach that you have seen in the past in other organizations or situations. If you are familiar with established change theory models, you can use the staged approach you're comfortable using, which will make the steps easy to follow.

One other aspect of this type of exercise is that it can also be used in a group setting, where the group has to discuss and agree the correct way forward. The same tips for gaining the right result apply, except you have to persuade other people to your way of thinking. This will be covered in Chapter 7.

TOP TIPS: Business case studies

1 Read the total brief and make appropriate notes as you read.

2 Consider the business objectives and the impact your actions will have on these.

3 Look for knock-on effects of your actions.

4 Work to the timescale and make time for a final check of the output.

5 Ensure you have covered all the required parts of the brief.

Self-evaluation

This seems like a strange subject to bring to an assessment centre. However, it is a facet of life that we are being regularly asked to consider. We are asked to look at how we are doing and what could we do better. In a business, you will usually have a form of appraisal once per year. In this process you will usually be required to highlight what you have achieved and identify areas for improvement, so it is not so unusual for us to have to evaluate ourselves.

These exercises will be used to identify your judgement, business acumen, decision making and critical thinking. The observers will have seen you at the event and will want to see if you can identify the real you and not an image of how you would like to be seen.

The observers will be looking at the following assessor essentials:

- good judgement of facts;
- correct evaluation of skills;
- correct evaluation of behaviours;
- a balance of positives and improvement areas;
- can see where the skills match business needs.

The two most common approaches for a self-evaluation exercise will be in the form of a report or a presentation. In some cases you may be expected to do both.

How to approach a self-evaluation exercise

We have already identified that this can be a difficult area to cover. However, it is important to be honest, as the observers will be matching your views with what they have observed. Don't be tempted either to hide where you think you need to develop, or to be falsely modest.

Hopefully you will find it fairly easy to identify what you do well. If you know you have a strength, don't downplay or hide it; remember that the observers will have seen your strengths in your performance during the other exercises. However, in an assessment centre setting, many people find their areas of improvement hard to face at times; it can feel difficult, like admitting that you are not perfect, when you want to be impressing your potential future employers! Remember, though, that no one is perfect and everyone can improve if they want to improve. All employers know that you will have improvement areas and will be pleased that you are able to identify these areas.

You can overcome any sense of negativity by stating the improvements that you feel are relevant and at the same time identifying either what you are currently doing to improve these, or what you would like to do to make the improvements. You are showing both self -awareness and a positive approach to the improvements. This is a professional approach which should be welcomed by any organization. In both the presentation and the report, however, although you should be honest about your development needs, you should still ensure that you balance your key contributions more highly than your development. After all, this is what you hope to bring to the role. End very positively and be confident in the delivery of this important message.

Practical examples

Let us now look at some of the ways this exercise will be executed.

EXAMPLE BRIEF: Self-evaluation report

You are required to complete a report of 1,000 words, representing how you see your strengths and improvement areas against the requirements of the job you have applied for.

You have 30 minutes to complete the exercise.

Good luck.

Such an exercise gives you an opportunity to outline what you feel you are good at. You need to ensure you are familiar with the job role prior to attending the event, because the key strengths you outline should relate to the requirements of the job role. In this way you can show you understand the requirements of the job and state your case by showing some key strengths in the critical areas you have identified. Then you need to show that you know you need to improve in certain areas and demonstrate how you will make the improvement happen, with an idea of timescales. Remember, everyone has improvement areas no matter what role they perform. Talk to any world-class athlete and they are always trying to improve, even if they are the best in the world!

This is a two-part exercise, ie strengths and improvements, so you need to cover both areas in the exercise. It is best to place more emphasis on strengths than on improvement areas, but to still show a rounded person who can see themselves clearly. Because it is a report, you can use the techniques from the section on written reports in Chapter 5.

EXAMPLE BRIEF: Self-evaluation presentation

You have applied for a role in the organization which is seen as pivotal to the success of the department over the next two years. You need to prepare a 10-minute presentation to outline how you will add to the value of the department by the way you will perform in the job role.

Consider any areas of your performance that will require further training or development.

In essence, this is a similar exercise to the previous example. It has two major parts: how you will contribute to the success of the department, and your training/development needs. You need to ensure you cover both of these areas. It is tempting to look at the contribution and believe you will not require any development (after all, if you didn't think you could do the job, you wouldn't have applied!), but try to think pragmatically and realistically. Even on the most basic level, you will need induction into the new company and orientation towards the job. So, try to be as honest as possible. You should show how you will contribute with your skills and behaviour against the job tasks, as well as how further training would make you even more effective. Trying to outline what sort of training you need, giving a timescale, will show that you have a good feel for your own development.

Practice: Self-evaluation

Take time to plan this exercise. Use the horizontal plan format to show your strengths and improvement areas, and show how the strengths relate to the job role.

TRY THIS: Self-evaluation

Complete an evaluation of your strengths and improvement areas and share the outcomes with a trusted friend or relative who knows you well. Ask them for feedback and for relevant examples they have seen of how you behave.

TOP TIPS: Self-evaluation

1 Use a clear structure for your work.

2 Outline what you do well and why it works.

3 Outline how to improve and what you will do.

4 Be honest in your approach.

5 Be confident in your approach.

Role-play exercises

These are exercises where the observers are trying to identify how you cope with other people when dealing with everyday issues. You will be dealing with issues that you have to raise with a staff member or problems an employee will raise with you. They want to see how you can cope in a strange situation where you only have your natural abilities of communication, problem solving and interpersonal skills to draw upon. These exercises will generally involve actors in the role of the employee; the actor will have been briefed to behave in a certain manner, to try to make you use your natural skills. The actors will know your brief, too, and will usually attempt to take you away from the main issues to identify if you have the resilience to see the issue through.

There are instances where people from the organization take on these acting roles, but it will usually not be the assessors, because they need to remain detached from the exercise and will be required for the observation of your performance. The assessor essentials for these exercises will be:

- establishes rapport with the staff member at the start;
- identifies the key issues;
- identifies any areas of difficulty;
- explores the detail of the issues;
- identifies any areas of difference and reasons;
- develops a clear way forward;
- agrees next action;
- agrees a follow-up if necessary;
- remains calm and controlled throughout;
- keeps control of the situation.

Role-play format

These exercises will usually have a general brief at the start to explain the situation you may face. It will outline who you will meet and who will attend. You may be in a group setting, watching each other's performance, or you may be assessed alone. If you are acting alone and your fellow candidates are not present, the exercise may last up to 30 minutes, and you will usually not get feedback on how you have done.

If you are in a group of people you will meet the actor or actors one at a time, and the exercise will only last about five minutes. The other candidates who are present will often be asked to give you feedback immediately after you have completed your role play, so you need to take notes of what happened in all the other candidates' role plays so that you can offer good feedback.

Where you are a group, you may have the same brief as every other candidate. However, the actor will perform differently on each exercise, so going last will give you little benefit as you will get a different approach from the actor to the others. This ensures everyone is tested equally.

Practical examples

Let us now look at a typical general brief you may receive.

EXAMPLE BRIEF: General role play

You will shortly be meeting a person you have not met before. They will be acting as a person from your team at work, and will have an issue you need to resolve.

    This is an individual exercise where you can demonstrate your people skills. Before you meet the individual you will be informed by the briefer about the issue they want to raise with you.

    You will be accompanied by your other colleagues, who will be required to take notes of your interaction. These notes will be used for a structured feedback session after every interaction. Each person will take part in the role play one after the other.

    Have you any questions?

The scene is now set for the exercises. Typically, if you receive a brief like this, you should also expect a more specific brief outlining the actual scenario. In this example, you will be given very little time to prepare, as the staff member is raising the issue; use the time you have to ensure you are ready for either silence or a tirade. And stay calm! We will look at a few techniques to respond to a range of possible situations so you can be ready for anything. Now let's look at some typical specific briefs.

EXAMPLE BRIEF: Staff member's issue role play

You are about to meet a member of your team who has e-mailed and asked to see you. The person has not said why they want to see you and you have no idea what the subject will be. You know the person is good at their job and expressed satisfaction with the company during the last performance review. The person is well established in their role and has worked for you for six years.

    Good luck.

This exercise can go anywhere as it is so open. The actor could be irate about a topic and try to dominate the situation; they may try to make personal attacks and claim you know about the issue but have been ignoring it; they may be passive aggressive or even reluctant to give you any detail at all. The main thing to remember is that the person has asked to see you and has not allowed you to prepare, therefore you cannot have instant answers. All you can do is explore the issues. To do this successfully, you need to remain calm and try to manage the conversation from the start. Don't worry if it's not easy to do so; remember, this is a role play, and is likely to be deliberately exaggerated.

Again, there are many resources available to develop your skills at managing difficult conversations, but some generally good advice for this type of scenario is to start by welcoming the other person and, for this example, asking what they want to discuss. After all, this is what their e-mail was about. After that let them talk, even if it is a tirade. Keep good notes and try to summarize what is said in a neutral manner. The aim is to have listened and understood the issue, so keep going with this until they can accept the summary, and then ask if there is anything else they wish to discuss.

Some helpful scripts might be:

- What is the issue as you see it?

- How long has this been going on?

- What effect has it had on you and your work?

- Has anyone else has seen this happen? Can you tell me who?

- Is there anything else on your mind at the moment?

These questions, or questions like it, are calm, neutral, and non-accusatory. They are aimed at helping you get all the information and establish facts. Only by getting the facts can you move forward, and this kind of question will encourage the person to give you this information rather than getting sidetracked too much by emotion (although in many situations, an emotional reaction is understandable and valid; this is why it is also important to let the person talk, even if it seems they are venting). However, if you allow them to dominate the conversation with all emotion and no fact, you can only go backwards, so if the person is aggressive or dominant, you need to stop that behaviour. Lowering your voice will help as it makes them have to try to hear what you are saying. You can also use various phrases and questions to redirect the person, such as:

- What do you want to see happen to take this away?
- How practical is your solution?
- What can I do to help you?
- Can we look at a set of actions we can adopt to move forward?
- Do you agree this is practical?
- When should we review progress?

In cases where the actor demonstrates extreme, out-of-control, or overtly aggressive or abusive behaviour, some strong phrases to shut this down would be appropriate, although your aim with the earlier questions and listening should always be to de-escalate and stop the situation developing that far. If it does, though, here are some useful questions and statements, to be delivered in an assertive, calm voice:

- Do you want my help to overcome this issue? If so, we need to act in a structured way.
- I understand your frustration, but we need to concentrate on the issue to be able to work together to overcome the problem.

In the example of the general brief above, the actor is raising an issue that you are not yet aware of. The other side of these role plays is where you have to address an issue with the other person, usually a personal issue related to behaviour or performance. With this type of exercise, you may get more time to prepare to deliver your views.

EXAMPLE BRIEF: Performance role play

You are about to meet a staff member who has started to be late for work. In the past six weeks they have been late on six separate occasions by more than one hour each time. This person is a good employee who has a perfect record of attendance over their six-year history with the company. You have to talk to them about the lateness.

When you know what the issue is, you are in control at the start, so the key is to retain control. Think about setting the tone. The actor (like most people in life!) will respond to what you say and how you say it, so your preparation needs to be structured and considerate of the other person. As a manager in this example, you have every right to talk to this person about the lateness issue. It is relevant to the role and will impact on how the person performs in their job. However, it is important to avoid being too critical and aggressive. This will not allow you to make progress, and the actor will either fail to respond and stay quiet or will attack back. Either way you will not make progress.

Just as we looked at in the feedback section of the last chapter, a better way is to get the other person talking. You need to put them at ease at the start and build rapport. For example, you could open by saying that you want a chat about their job and then asking how they feel it is going. You can ask if they are having any difficulties at work, which may allow them to raise the lateness themselves. If that does not work, you need to outline that you have a concern about their lateness and want to help. Again, being calm, non-accusatory and direct is important (don't fudge around the issue to be 'kind', as this only makes the conversation feel awkward for everyone). This will hopefully lead to a discussion about the real cause, and you will then be able to identify what can be done to help. For this particular example, we know that the lateness is new and unusual for this person, which suggests that the problem will be temporary, and something you are able to assist with.

Here are some short scripts that could be useful in this exercise:

- Good morning, how are you?
- How is the job going at the moment?
- Are there any issues I can help with at the moment?
- I have noticed that you have struggled to get to work on time recently.
- This is not like you, is there any help you need at the moment?
- What is causing the lateness?
- How long will that be an issue?

- What can we do to help you overcome the problem?
- Will X help you?
- Can we agree that we will do X over the next few weeks?
- Let's review this to ensure it is helping you.
- Do you want others to be aware of what we have agreed?
- Thanks for your input.
- Feel free to come and see me if the problem changes.

Scripts like this can lead to a positive outcome. The conversation recognizes that you want to keep a good staff member and are prepared to accommodate their needs providing it is not too disruptive. The questions allow the person to talk about what's going on without making it a 'telling off', and focus on practical resolutions, using inclusive language like 'we'. It also acknowledges the person's otherwise good track record and makes allowance for that.

Another approach for this type of exercise could be dealing with a personal issue. Again, as a manager, you have the responsibility to tackle issues that affect the job and the working climate.

EXAMPLE BRIEF: Personal issue role play

You have a team member with two years' service who appears to have a personal hygiene problem. They have body odour, an issue which is starting to be raised by other staff members. These staff members do not want to work alongside this person due to the unpleasant smell.

　You have to tackle this issue with the individual.

Clearly, this is not a pleasant task and can so easily go wrong. To do nothing is not an option; however, you need to have a degree of sensitivity for the person's feelings. If you are too blunt you will upset them. If you are too casual or vague about the issue, it will not be taken seriously and the problem won't be solved.

In the other examples, we have looked at how to start by engaging with the person to see if they raise this as a problem; for something as potentially awkward and personal as this, it's even more important to do so. Then you should outline what you have found from a personal angle. Really key for this particular scenario is to remember that there is no need to mention the other people, as it may cause even more embarrassment for the individual. You need a practical solution for the problem that the individual owns. In most cases, the person is unaware of the issue or feels it is not too much of a problem, so you need to explain the consequences of the continuation of the problem. Remembering that in a role play, the actor will likely be deliberately trying to make it a harder task for you, most actors will go off on a tangent about their feelings, refuse to engage with the conversation, or take offence and blame you for insensitivity. You need to be prepared to listen but always bring the person back to the practical impact of the issue.

Here are some short scripts that could be useful in this exercise:

- Good morning.

- How are you?

- How are you feeling today?

- I'd like to talk to you about something. I've noticed that recently there is a distinct smell of body odour that seems to be coming from you or your clothes.

- I would hate for this to become something that distracts from your excellent work and great relationships with the team.

- I want to stress that this is between you and me, and I don't want you to feel embarrassed about this.

- Are you aware of this issue?

- What are the causes? Is everything alright with you generally?

- How can I help?

- What are you going to do to alleviate the problem?

- Agree clear actions.

- When should we review this?

- Wish the person well.

- Stress that you are here to help if they need it.

This script will help address the issues you face. Always keep a focus on what you have to do, as you are the manager. You have a duty to deal with the problem, as well as look out for the welfare of your team member. Notice that in these scripts, the language is clear and direct. The tone you use will matter a great deal, as it will mean the difference between sounding excruciatingly awkward (making it worse for your staff member) or accusatory (causing them to feel more defensive than necessary), and sounding kind and matter of fact, which will allow the person to save face as much as possible. Just like the other scenarios, the conversation is considerate of emotion, and allows space for the person to have their say, but ultimately focuses on moving forward with practical actions.

The final type of role play will involve the candidate in a one-to-one session with either an actor or a company manager. This will involve looking at a real issue and developing a solution. You will often find this exercise used where you will have to use interview type skills or coaching in the role. The exercise will allow you to show what you can do in a 'real' situation. Organizations will use a current situation to explore just how good your skills are in dealing with real problems, and the use of a current manager will enhance the brief, as they have all the facts and will not need to be pre-briefed by the company.

EXAMPLE BRIEF: Real situation role play

You will be meeting a manager of X department in 15 minutes. This manager has a problem with the current operation of their department.

You have to establish what the current problem with their department is and help them identify potential practical solutions that can be considered for use in the future. You will have 30 minutes with the manager to complete the brief.

This is a short brief, but it has two main elements to create success. First, you have to identify the problem in the department, then you need to help the manager identify potential solutions. As you know nothing about the issues or the department you will need to ask many relevant questions to get the facts. You are likely to need to use a coaching style to get what you need. For this to work effectively, you will need to create a rapport with the manager before you get into the detail of the issues. You can do this by looking first at the structure and background of the department, before moving on to the more relevant areas of the brief. This will help you when you get into details.

Here are some suggested scripts to help you open the conversation and create rapport:

- Good morning, I am X, and I have done Y in the past.
- I believe you have a few issues in your department you would like to discuss with me.
- Could we please look at the structure and function of the department first?

Now some questions that may help you establish the current issues:

- What are the main issues you face as a department?
- What effect do these have on the overall organization?
- What has caused these issues to arise?
- What has changed over the last few months?
- How do you feel about these issues?
- What will the department look like when these issues are solved?
- What will prevent these issues being solved?
- Whose help will you need to be successful?

And finally, these scripts may help you agree potential solutions:

- What do we need to do to develop effective solutions?
- Who will be involved in these solutions?
- What are the advantages of each solution?
- What are the downsides of each solution?
- How can we minimize the downsides?
- Which would be your preferred solution?
- Why is it that one?
- What assistance would you need to implement the solution?
- Who would you need to involve?

- What would you need in order to communicate the solution?
- How would you gain commitment from the team?
- What would be the timescale of the implementation?
- How would the organization see the success?

Just like in the other examples, the person you are dealing with is likely to try to make things difficult for you. In this case, they may have been told to only answer the questions you ask, and not to help you, as the observer is interested in how you would work normally. This means that for exercises like this example, you should not expect the person to be overly willing to give details. You will need to work to get at the relevant information; be very inquisitive and assume nothing. Check out your assumptions with the other person to ensure you have the right information.

As you can see, you need to look deeply at the issues and not just accept any answer. By taking your time and coaching out answers you will get to the real issues and develop real solutions. This will impress the observer, who will see that you can build rapport and generate good solutions to real problems. These are qualities and skills you can take back to work and apply in the actual situation.

Practice: Role play

Try out using some of the role-play exercises with a family member or trusted colleague. Try to use your words to become more familiar with the approach to a problem When completed, ask for relevant feedback.

TOP TIPS: Role play

1 Stay calm and do not react negatively.

2 Keep control of the situation.

3 Get the other person talking but keep to the topic.

4 Don't allow the person to take control.

5 Get the all the information before you move forward.

Key points to remember

1 Whatever exercise is used, stay calm.

2 Consider all the options that are available to you in the exercise.

3 Ensure you relate your solutions to the business goals.

4 If working with others, get the other person involved in the conversation.

5 Clarify the final position to ensure you have a long-term solution.

07
Group exercises

We have just looked at the most common type of exercise – individual exercises – used at assessment centres. We now need to spend time on the group exercises, which are the next most likely type of exercise that will be employed in an assessment centre.

These exercises will have many formats but will usually be for groups of between five and 10 candidates. They are used to establish how you work in a group, allowing you to demonstrate your competency with verbal communication, interpersonal skills, teamwork, leadership, judgement, tenacity and usually problem solving. This is quite a spectrum of competencies, and that is why such exercises are used. Group exercises will normally be in the form of the following:

- group discussions;
- problem solving – practical exercises;
- problem solving – theoretical exercises;
- life or death decision making;
- follow-up exercises.

The typical assessor essentials for this type of exercise will cover a wide area; however, there are a few assessor essentials that will be in almost every situation you face:

- aware of the expected outcome;
- shared views freely with the group;
- listened to other views and acted when necessary;
- encouraged others to take part;
- led the group at times;
- group listened to the views you expressed;

- planned the task;
- organized the group effort towards the goal;
- recognized positive inputs from others;
- reviewed end product against the exercise requirements;
- re-planned if task went wrong.

The OPPOSE model

During these exercises you may feel you are more likely to make a mistake as the content is strange and you are working with other people. Do not despair if a mistake happens, as you will be able to rectify it and you will get a further opportunity to demonstrate your skills in this and other exercises. If it is the last exercise, you will have already demonstrated these skills in other exercises. Remember too that the other team members are there to assist in the success of the task, and it is in their interest to rectify any area where you feel you have made a mistake. Most people are over-sensitive about what they see as mistakes and tend to blow them out of all proportion. Stay focused on what needs to be done and forget any errors, as you will now rectify them as a group. You need to get a clear focus on the task and ensure you plan how it will be achieved.

As most of these exercises will involve the interaction of the group in some form of meeting, you will need a strategy to cope with these meetings and help you avoid mistakes in the first place. One approach is the OPPOSE approach – a much more positive model than the name suggests! This approach can be summarized as:

O – Objective
P – Positive approach
P – Plan
O – Offer views
S – Support the team and individuals
E – Evaluate the progress and outcome

Let us look at how this oppose approach will operate for you to gain success in most types of group exercise, so you are able to demonstrate what the assessor is looking for. You will need to consider each of these areas during the exercise.

Objective. I cannot stress too strongly that you need to be clear about what you are being asked to achieve in the exercise. You need to clarify what you understand to be the objective and ask relevant questions to strengthen your understanding. Once you know what you have to achieve you can gain success. If you do not know what you have to achieve you will never be confident in gaining the success you require in the exercise. This is true of all your activities at an assessment centre, but even more so for group tasks. Once you are clear on the objective you need to then ensure the team sees this as clearly as you. Spend time making sure that the objective is clear to all, as this is what you all have to be working towards as a group.

Positive. Your approach to all the exercises needs to be positive at all times, even if the task goes wrong. You should demonstrate your confidence in your ability to succeed. Again, this is true of all the tasks, but it can be more challenging to maintain a positive approach if, for example, you are frustrated by the other members of the group, or if they have a nervous or negative attitude. If the group are negative about the task, you can try to talk them into a positive mood by stressing your confidence in the exercise. Being positive with the individuals in the group and their ideas will demonstrate that you are a team player. Listen to others' views carefully and respond with what you like and only then outline any areas you believe are difficult to overcome. This is a positive approach and demonstrates that you listen carefully.

Plan. The key to success in most exercises is to spend time planning how to achieve the objective. By utilizing this time effectively, you will be able to consider a number of relevant options and agree a joint way forward. The plan should include the identified solution as well as who will do what activity and when it will be achieved. This creates a co-ordinated approach that will lead to success.

You will usually find that some team members don't want to plan, as they just want to get on with the task. In this case, you want to be seen as the person who is leading the need to plan, as, without a plan, the task will usually fail. Try to get the total involvement of the group in the plan, and even if some want to start and refuse to plan, try to influence the others to stay focused. Even if you are overruled, you will have shown the assessors the correct approach.

Offer views. In these group exercises it is important that you outline your views along with the relevant benefits of your proposed action. By taking your time to state your views clearly, the team members are more likely to understand your position; they will not always accept your idea, but by having an idea and speaking up about it – even by advocating for it to a certain level if there is resistance – you will have demonstrated your clear communication, problem solving, and appropriate assertiveness to the assessors.

Support. You will be trying to sell your idea to the group, and naturally the group will also individually sell their ideas. You should listen to the ideas and respond according to how you perceive them. If the idea is adopted by the group, show your support for the way forward. This will show that you are flexible and adaptable to change.

You also need to show your support for individuals who are struggling to get air time for their views. By attempting to involve them in the plans or ideas you will show that you are a team player who supports team members. You can easily demonstrate this by asking the quieter members of the team what they think of the ideas or asking them if they have any other ideas.

Evaluate. With any plan, there comes a time to review progress to ensure the end product will be delivered on time and to specification. Such reviews are crucial as they allow time to make amendments to the plan and ensure the successful completion of the exercise.

Then, at the end of the exercise, it is useful to review how the exercise went. Did it follow the plan and deliver the required results? You can identify any areas for improvement, which will help if you work with this group again or have to complete the exercise again at a later stage.

By carrying out a review you are able to demonstrate that you are not only interested in the result but have a concern for the process utilized to gain success. You often face resistance to this review from one or more team members, but don't let that stop you from trying to look at how to improve. All organizations appreciate a person who wants to be better at what they do.

You now have a process to follow for these exercises, so let us look at the different types of exercise in more detail as it will give a closer look at how to perform better than the other candidates. It is worth spending time on these exercises as they can be used a lot in the assessment process.

Group discussions

This is where the candidates are selected to work with the others in a group. The group will normally be given a brief to follow that will outline what you have to do to complete the task successfully. Such exercises are best handled in two parts.

You are given time to prepare your ideas and then share them with the group. The group then has to discuss and agree a way forward, the key phrase being discuss and agree. This means that you are expected as a group to listen to each other's ideas and develop them further. You also have to agree as a group the best way forward.

The time limit is important as at times a failure to reach an agreement means that no idea is adopted. This is seen as failure to agree, as one aspect of the brief is not met.

The assessor essentials for this type of exercise will include:

- understood the brief;
- prepared effectively during the individual part of the exercise;
- developed an agreed plan to tackle the problem;
- presented own ideas effectively;
- listened to the comments of others and responded appropriately;
- listened to others' ideas;
- took an active part in the discussion;
- involved others in the process;
- checked that the final position matched the required outcome.

Practical examples

We now need to look at some typical exercises you could face so that we can show how it works.

EXAMPLE BRIEF: Group discussion

You have a budget of £10,000, which has to be allocated to one business project.

You have to prepare a case for a new product or service for the company. You have 10 minutes to prepare your case.

The group will have 30 minutes to discuss and agree the product or service which gets the £10,000.

If you cannot agree, the money will be lost.

If we look at the exercise example it shows what you are required to achieve within a time limit. Failure to complete the task within the timescale leads to all the money being lost. This looks like a simple brief, but it becomes complex as each person will have a totally different idea to move forward and only one idea can be used. Therefore, it will be necessary to develop a plan at the start of the exercise to tackle the problem.

In exercises like this example, there will usually be someone in the team that believes they have the answer, making the need to plan obsolete. Following this path will usually lead to disaster, as the team becomes dependent on the person being right. In my experience, I normally see such a person trying to dominate the process, which will leave the rest of the group surplus to requirements. When this happens, everyone will fail to impress the observer as there will be little discussion and agreeing – and this will include the person with the original idea. We will look at how to deal with a dominating group member in more detail in Chapter 10.

So, by setting a plan you allow everyone to input within a time limit. The group also needs to decide how to select the best idea; simply voting for your favourite might be easy but is rarely the most effective approach. One way to do this is to agree criteria to measure the response of the group to the different ideas. There should be at least three criteria, so that some or most ideas can be eliminated, and these can be very simple. For this example, you might choose:

1 Is the idea practical? (ie it has a good chance of working.)

2 Does the idea deliver a benefit to the whole business?

3 Will it cost no more than £10,000? (Will it meet all of the brief?)

4 Is it easy to implement?

Each idea can be evaluated against these criteria. Each group member – or even the group as a whole – puts a tick against the criterion if it is met, and a cross if it is not met (see Table 7.1). In this way the group talks about the feasibility of the different strands of the idea. You will get more discussion centred around how the idea measures up to the criteria, meaning it will be relevant and focused on what you need to achieve.

Table 7.1 Criteria example

Criteria	IDEA				
	1	2	3	4	5
Practical	✓	✓	✓	✗	✓
Delivers	✗	✗	✓	✗	✓
Costs £10,000 or less	✗	✓	✓	✓	✓
Easy to implement	✓	✗	✓	✓	✗

You can see from Table 7.1 that only idea 3 meets all the criteria; therefore, it will be selected as it has the approval of the group. If you need a fallback option, it will be the next best option; idea 5 in this example has only one cross and all the other ideas have more crosses. If two ideas pass all the criteria steps, the team can then discuss which they feel is best to propose as the solution.

If you take an active part in planning how to succeed and propose the criteria approach you will stand out from the rest. The key, though, is to be assertive and collaborative; the person who tries to dominate will not be seen as a team player and will not get far in this process. You do not need to be a dominator.

You also do not need to argue with a dominator; tackle them with questions about their approach. A suggested script might be, 'What you are proposing sounds good; however, we are supposed to discuss and agree and that can only be achieved by all of us having an equal say.' This is an assertive but not aggressive approach. Even if the others end up wanting to follow the dominator, you will have stood out as an assertive person who was aligned to the goals of the exercise. (We will look at how to deal with dominating people in more detail in Chapter 10.)

Emotive discussions

A variation on the quite open-ended example above is to link the discussion to an area that may have an emotional tie with some or all of the individuals in the group. This will attempt to see who can discuss and agree without letting their emotions get in the way of a good decision. While passion for a cause can be a great thing, and can be motivating and make you a valuable candidate, too often people believe that because something is close to their heart it should be close to everyone's heart. This causes them to be blinkered and not listen to others. Such people fail to impress the observers as their enthusiasm tends to overshadow the efforts of others due to their domination. Here is an example of this kind of group discussion exercise:

EXAMPLE BRIEF: Emotive group discussion

You have to select a national charity which will receive a £1,000 donation from the company. You must select a charity and develop a rationale as to why the money should be given to this organization.

You will be required to discuss and agree with others which charity will receive the money. You have 10 minutes to prepare your case.

You will be rated on your arguments rather than the moral value of the charity.

The money can only go to one charity and simply voting on the donations is not allowed.

Most people will have some favourite charity, and this can be closely linked to real-life experience and deep-running emotions. This can lead the team to stray from the brief by failing to discuss and agree;

all too often some team members will talk too much about personal experiences to the exclusion of others' views. People may refuse to support others' views because they feel they are right. It is also a problem that sometimes occurs when two people favour the same charity, as they can sometimes form a sub-group and set themselves in opposition to the others in the group. However, neither will benefit from such an arrangement, as again it prevents discussion and agreement.

With such a subject, it is most important to have a starting plan and develop how each person can share their views. The criteria approach used in the previous exercise will help make the decision without the vote and can overcome the emotions if you have agreed the criteria at the start.

Business experience tasks

On occasion you will be required to discuss and agree a subject that the whole group will have some experience of, although these experiences will be different, and at times opposing. Unlike the deliberately emotive tasks explored above, such topics are usually of a business nature and can relate directly to the job being offered. Let us look at a typical example of this approach.

EXAMPLE BRIEF: Business experience group discussion

You are about to attend a meeting with other people at the assessment centre. You have 10 minutes to prepare for this meeting.

You will need to discuss and agree an induction and training programme for the role of a new manager. You need to assume that the manager is new to the organization and has some experience of managing people. This should focus on what needs to be done to ensure any candidate will be successful in the new role. Consider your own experience and what has worked in the past. It is also useful to examine what you would like to have happened in the past.

The meeting has 30 minutes to reach a conclusion.

This is a very straightforward brief. You have individual preparation time as well as a discussion time with the group which is adequate for the subject. Most people will have some views on induction and will have some relevant experience they can share. This should lead to a good discussion involving the total group. To be successful, you need to ensure time is divided between the discussion of the details and the final agreement of the programme. This will make sure you achieve the objective. As it is a wide topic you will be able to allow everyone's ideas to be incorporated into the final programme. This should lead to less conflict than in the previous example.

This is an exercise where you should try to take a lead and guide the group through the plan of how they will work towards the final position. Ensure you get ideas from the total group, as all individuals have had 10 minutes' preparation time. In such exercises it is useful to use any aids such as whiteboards or flipcharts to record the progress you are making as a team. This is a motivator for the group as they can readily see progress, and shows what still needs to be developed to gain the final objective. Be aware, though; if you are the person using the board, ensure you only record what is agreed. There is a tendency for people to record what they think will be in line with their ideas, but this will lead to conflict when the group realize what you are doing, and the observer will see this, which would not be in your favour.

How to approach a group discussion

You may want to look at these group discussion exercises as a form of meeting. There are two ways in which the chairperson of a meeting will succeed: the first is to ensure every person has a fair say and is not interrupted when they are making their points, and the second is to manage the time in order to achieve the brief. It is too easy to be caught up in the heat of the arguments and not realize that no progress is being made. You have to manage the group towards a final decision.

With all the briefs you receive you need to take time to understand what is required from the exercise. The observer is looking mainly at the process you are following rather than how good your idea may be.

The observer wants to see a person who respects others' views and is assertive with their ideas. This will be helped if you involve others and ask for their views. Being supportive of others who have a good idea will be seen as good judgement as well as supportive behaviour.

You need to manage your individual preparation time to get the most benefit for you and the task. Take time to consider what needs to be done and your ideas or main points. Use some of the time to consider how the process of the task should work and the blockages you may encounter. By planning this aspect of the task and sharing it with the group, you will be seen in a positive light. You will be observed as being able to plan and organize as well as influence the group.

You can demonstrate your interpersonal skills, verbal communication, teamwork, leadership and problem-solving skills in these exercises. Remember to think broadly about the exercise, as it is designed so that you can demonstrate your skills. Don't fall into the negative traps that others may fall into such as arguing too much or refusing to listen to others' ideas; as with every exercise, be as positive as you can about the ideas coming from other participants rather than being dismissive. Look for how they can be made to work rather than why they will not work.

TOP TIPS: Group discussions

1 Always work towards the objective.

2 Make your points clearly and stress any benefits.

3 Listen to others and involve the quiet people.

4 Use the criteria approach to evaluate ideas.

5 Keep a close eye on the time available.

Problem-solving activities

These exercises by their nature require the team to make, construct or perform a practical task. The brief will have a problem or task that will need to be delivered in a specific timescale and with various criteria attached. You will be given various materials and will be asked to use only those materials to deliver an output. Such tasks will seem difficult if not impossible to some of the group. Be advised that these tasks can almost always be done and in a number of different ways, even if they seem tricky. However you may feel about the task, always remain positive and focused on what can be done.

These exercises will be used to identify your skills in working with people, leadership, teamwork, problem solving, decision making, influencing and verbal communications. This will cover a lot of skills, so it is an ideal opportunity to demonstrate how you work and how you influence other people. The typical assessor essentials that they will be identifying with these exercises will be:

- understands the objective of the exercise;
- plans what has to be done to achieve the objective;
- agrees a plan with all involved;
- listens attentively to others' views;
- allocates people to various tasks;
- co-ordinates the efforts of the group to achieve the objective;
- reviews progress regularly;
- re-plans the work if necessary;
- praises the work of the team;
- completes any task that is allocated;
- remains enthusiastic about the task and the teamwork.

Practical examples

Most of the tasks you are given are completed indoors, yet some organizations will set tasks to be completed in an outdoor setting. This should not lead you to be concerned. If this is the case, you will often be warned in advance and asked to bring outdoor shoes. If you are not pre-warned, the organization will provide suitable clothing. The outdoor exercises are the same as the indoor exercises except for the environment. The assessor essentials will be the same. Let us first look at an exercise that can be used both indoors and outdoors.

Transport an object to the ground

A common task is to transport an egg or similar breakable object from a height to the ground without breaking it. It may be suspended from a light fitting in a room or from a tree branch if you are working outdoors. Most people will not have encountered such a problem, so the group have to use whatever ideas they have to complete the exercise correctly.

EXAMPLE BRIEF: Egg time

You have the task of successfully transporting a suspended egg safely to the ground without it breaking. The egg must be in contact with the ground on completion. You will be shown the site of the egg by the briefer.

The only materials you can use will be flipchart paper and sticky tape. You have to decide the cost of completing this exercise, and this estimate is required 10 minutes from the commencement of the exercise.

The cost of the flipchart paper is £10 per sheet and the roll of tape is £20.

Whatever you construct must be free-standing, ie no one or thing can touch the final structure (except the ground). You cannot attach anything to the egg or touch the egg.

The total time for the exercise is 30 minutes.

You will see from the example that it appears to be straightforward; don't break the egg when you drop it onto the floor. However, if you read the brief properly you will see that there are actually two tasks. One is to bring the egg down safely; the other is to give a cost estimate within 10 minutes. This means that you need to have a plan that is fully costed within 10 minutes, leaving 20 minutes to complete the practical task. Your best bet is to ensure the planning is completed early, but don't fall into the trap of just making up an estimate, as the observer may insist that you complete the exercise with only the materials required. They may also ask you to keep a record of costs and then compare this with the estimate at the end. These requirements are not in the original brief but may be added as you progress through the exercise. Such techniques are used to ensure you plan properly and deliver to the original plan.

Apart from this, there are a number of things that regularly go wrong with this type of exercise. The main one is a lack of ideas or having only one idea at the start, so try to get at least two good ideas to compare at the start. Often a mixture of the ideas will be the real solution. You often get a dominator in this exercise who believes they alone have the answer. Make sure you do not allow the person to take the group forward until other ideas are exhausted – we will look at this more in Chapter 10. You may also get a person who feels the task cannot be done or is stupid. Try to bring the person into the group without letting them pull you into this negative attitude. This exercise can be done, like all the others you will face.

Whilst there may be many possible answers to the problem you are set, always take due regard of the rules imposed on the task. In this example, the structure must be free-standing, nothing is to touch the structure and you cannot attach anything to the egg. Be certain to abide by these rules. If you don't take these into consideration, it will appear that you have not understood the task. In some instances, the observer will tell you your structure does not comply but will fail to say why. This causes confusion and in some cases frustration. To deal with this, at the start of the exercise it is best to clarify what you can and cannot do. Ask the briefer of the task to explain their version of free-standing etc. This avoids panic at a later stage when the whole idea has depended upon something you cannot do.

Spanning structures

A commonly used exercise is to ask the team to build a structure that will span a gap, given limited resources and time. Such an exercise can be fun but also frustrating if it does not go well. We need to look at a typical example of this to fully understand what may be required.

EXAMPLE BRIEF: A bridge too far

You have as a team to construct a bridge out of flipchart paper and sticky tape. The bridge has to be free-standing, ie it cannot rest on anything (except the floor) and cannot be held in place.

The bridge must be nine feet long and can have a maximum of six legs. It must also have a minimum height of 2'6" at its lowest point. When completed the bridge must stand for two minutes and support a marker pen in the middle of any span.

You have 30 minutes to complete this task. The cost of sticky tape is £10 per metre, and flipchart paper is £6 per sheet. You have to give a cost estimate no later than 15 minutes after the start of the exercise. You also need to order the materials at this stage and then commence the build. Any items built prior to the estimate being required will be withdrawn and hence cannot be used.

This task is similar to the egg exercise, but there are some subtle differences. This is a permanent structure that must stand for two minutes and needs a lot of planning. The main difference you will see by reading carefully is that there is a new parameter in place; you cannot build the bridge until you have given your estimate. It states that anything you build prior to the estimate will be removed. You can plan and make a similar bridge, but you have to start again using the materials you order.

This often catches a group out. They believe they are part way to a solution when the observer takes away their good work. In some cases I have seen anger and other people have withdrawn from the team because they think it is unfair. Be clear about the brief and this will not happen.

This exercise has many variations. The most common one is to ask for a bridge that is a replica of an existing bridge, eg The Tyne Bridge or Tower Bridge. The replica will possibly be related to the area of the country you are currently in. Another variation is to build a structure that represents a tower such as the Shard or a monument such as the Angel of the North. Let us now look at a typical example of such an exercise.

EXAMPLE BRIEF: Tyne Bridge

You have to build a replica of the Tyne Bridge from flipchart paper and sticky tape. The bridge must be at least three feet from the ground at its mid-point and be free-standing from the floor. The structure needs to be at least six feet in length. When completed, the mid-point must be able to hold the weight of three golf balls.

You need to provide the tutor with a plan of what you intend to build and a breakdown of resources required. These will be supplied and need to be monitored to see how close you get to your plan. You cannot build the bridge until you have supplied your plan.

You have 30 minutes to complete the task.

Good luck.

Whatever the variation in the exercise you need to be practical in your approach and read the brief carefully. Ensure you are clear about what you have to achieve and plan the task using all of the team. You will find various solutions to this type of exercise on the internet.

Restart tasks

There are exercises that will be different in that, in addition to the fixed resources and strict rules, you have to start again from the beginning if the exercise goes wrong or you breach the rules. The rules and brief will be similar in most instances. Let us look at a typical example.

EXAMPLE BRIEF: Restart

Your task is to transport a ball from one side of the room to the other in a structured manner. You cannot just throw the ball. You need to construct a method to ensure the ball never touches the floor and is never less than three feet from the floor. You cannot touch the ball when it is on its journey, and your team cannot be within three feet of the ball when it is on its journey.

You have the following materials:

- a ball of string;
- a bag;
- one roll of sticky tape;
- two canes;
- a flipchart pad;
- a ruler.

You may only use the materials supplied. If you try to move the ball and it touches the ground or is less than three feet from the ground at any time, you have to restart the task. You will only get a maximum of three attempts.

You have **30** minutes to complete the task.

Good luck.

In this example you have to transport a ball without touching the ground or floor using fixed resources. It may seem easy but there will be some difficulties you may not have planned to encounter; when you see the restart clause in an exercise, this is a clue that it may not be as simple to deliver as it looks, and mistakes will be made.

The restart usually comes from a team member (or the whole team) not understanding the brief. It is essential when you are briefed to gain full clarification of what will cause a restart. You need to ensure the restart items or rules are in the team's mind by restating them before you start each attempt. In these exercises, it is most important to evaluate the plan after each restart. Most teams just start again and hope to succeed, so re-planning will set you aside from other candidates. You need to know why you failed and how to overcome the problem in the future before you restart. This exercise can be easily used both indoors and outdoors, and will be fun to take part in as long as you re-plan after each failure.

How to approach problem-solving activities

Due to time constraints, these tasks are not always completed. This is not a major disadvantage to any group, as the observer is looking at the process you adopt and the interaction of the group. So, you can impress the observer even if the task is incomplete. Sometimes it becomes obvious near the end that the task will not be completed correctly. It is best in that circumstance to start to re-plan how to make a success of the exercise. This may seem like a waste of time but it will show that you are still focused on the task and want to succeed. Too often groups go into panic mode and try without thought to rectify a mistake. This rarely works and looks to an observer like panic and an unstructured approach.

As you can see from the examples, most of these exercises will employ materials like flipchart paper, photocopy paper, staples and sticky tape. These are used because they are easy to use and most people will be familiar with them. Paper is much stronger than you think. When you make paper into a cylinder it will hold a good weight. However, when you try to join it to other paper, it can be weak at the joint, and will need reinforcement to become strong again. This is where tape and staples can be used.

A final typical exercise most people may have seen is to make a paper tower from photocopier paper and staples that is eight feet tall from the ground. Using cylinders from the photocopier paper that are stapled with a sheet of paper between each layer will yield a positive result. You can make the cylinder stronger by making the diameter smaller so that the sheet is rolled up tight.

TOP TIPS: Problem-solving activities

1 Ensure you understand what has to be achieved and the full constraints of the exercise.

2 Develop a plan of action to achieve the objective, so each person knows their role.

3 Regularly check the progress of the task against the timescale.

4 Ensure everyone is involved in the planning and delivery phases of the exercise.

5 If the plan is not working, be prepared to re-plan to achieve the objective.

Problem-solving theoretical exercises

This sort of exercise is usually based around a decision regarding recruitment or donation to charity. It is more of a meeting format – like the group discussions – but will have some key variations. The exercises will have a degree of individual preparation time followed by a deadline to make a decision. The content of the brief will be one you will be able to relate to and have a relevant view on.

These exercises will test skills or competencies in leadership, teamwork, interpersonal skills, influencing, problem solving and decision making.

The typical assessor essentials that are required will be:

- plans for the task;
- communicates ideas freely and effectively;
- listens actively to others' views;
- discusses others' views;
- identifies the objective and helps the team work towards it;
- influences other members of the group with solid arguments;
- prepared to agree a route forward;
- looks at alternative approaches;
- makes decisions based on facts;
- works within the timeframe allocated;
- makes the group aware of time and progress;
- reviews progress regularly.

Practical examples

It is useful to look at some typical examples of the type of exercises you may face. With all of these exercises, underline the issues as you find them; especially the objective of the exercise. Look at each and make relevant notes to remind you of what is important. This will save time re-reading the brief later.

EXAMPLE BRIEF: Problem solving

During this exercise you must make group decisions regarding three situations at work. You will need to refer to the case outlines for each situation. You should voice your perceptions and ideas and contribute to the final group decision of what action should be taken. Also identify how you would address the issue.

All three decisions must be completed and posted on the flipchart within 20 minutes.

Case 1

Employee name: Mike Taylor   **Performance**: Good
Current job: Planning Manager   **Length of service**: 30 years

Situation: Mike has been with the organization in his current role for two years. In that time he has performed well. He is experienced in planning with this organization but has not worked in other organizations.

In the last 12 months the organization has been working towards developing a new computerized approach to planning. It is felt that such an approach will enhance the level of customer service and also involve less time in paperwork.

Whilst Mike likes the idea of enhancing the performance of the department, he has been negative about the computer system. He feels that two extra people would provide a better service level.

He has also missed a number of meetings with the consultants who will install the system.

In more recent times he has behaved badly at team meetings and has not offered the right level of support to the team of his colleagues.

How will you handle this situation?

Case 2

Employee name: John Dunn   **Performance**: Too new to tell
Current job: Trainee   **Length of service**: Eight weeks

Situation: John has not settled well into the company. In the last eight weeks he has been late one day per week. On each occasion he has claimed he slept in and was sorry.

Most of the work he has done has been satisfactory. He is operating the photocopier and delivering mail. He appears to be getting on well with his colleagues and seems to know where each person is situated in the building.

At interview, John was very positive and seemed to want this job. Since joining the company he seems negative and rarely smiles. Some managers have commented that he does not appear to like the job.

Today one of John's colleagues commented that they were 'sick of hearing him moan'.

How will you handle this situation?

Case 3

Employee name: Jane Craig   **Performance**: Superior
Current job: IT Specialist   **Length of service**: Eight years

Situation: Jane is well respected by her colleagues and most of the managers in the organization. She is seen as a person who is positive and achieves results. In the last few years she has made a tremendous contribution to the company and introduced a lot of IT solutions that have saved both time and money.

Recently you have talked to Jane about her future in the company. She was surprised to talk about this as she feels she is doing what she wants to do and does not want to move into another job. She has great job satisfaction and regards this as a major plus point of the job.

Some of the directors are so pleased with her work that they want to promote her to a managerial role. They see her as having great potential.

How will you handle this situation?

This is a typical exercise which looks at three different situations in a working environment. You will be asked to offer your view on each situation. The situations are fairly common to most organizations. There is no right solution to these issues as you only have a small amount of information. In essence, the brief is asking you to identify how you would tackle the three situations to get a positively motivated staff member. As you can see, there is a tight time limit on this exercise (20 minutes). Therefore, as a group you need to be smart and quick to address the issues and complete the task on time.

You will note that there is one additional task other than discussing, and that is to post the group answers on a flipchart by the end of the 20 minutes. This additional task is an integral part of the exercise to ascertain if the group are focused on the total exercise or get trapped by the main discussion. Ensure the decisions are recorded as the group progresses. This stops a panic at the end.

During the exercise you need to:

- Ensure there is a process for finding the solution.

- Set a short planning time: for example, simply agree to spend six minutes on each case and record the answers as you go, identifying who will keep time and who will record the answers. This will show you know what has to be done and how it can be achieved.

- Ensure that you remain time-conscious.

- Ensure that you share your views.

- Be aware if someone has not spoken during the exercise and ask them how they see the situation.

- Listen at all times to what is being said.

One other way to tackle the exercise is to set up three groups, with each group looking at a separate problem and feeding back their views to the whole group. This solution can then be enhanced by a focused discussion with the whole group. It may speed up the process, but it will not show too much teamwork or influencing until the whole group meets.

Selecting the right person

A common exercise is to be asked to select a suitable person for a job or place potential candidates in a rank order. This is where you will be given a series of person profiles to discuss as a group. In almost all of these cases you will be given personal time to prepare before the discussion. You need to use the time to become familiar with the details and make appropriate notes on the profiles.

EXAMPLE BRIEF: Pub manager selection

You are going to attend a meeting with your colleagues. You have to review the CVs of the enclosed candidates for the role of Regional Manager for a group of 30 public houses. These have been supplied to you by a recruitment agency as a suitable shortlist. You can assume that salary and location are not a problem in this recruitment.

You have 10 minutes to prepare for a meeting with your colleagues. At the meeting you have to discuss and agree the rank order of the candidates from most suitable to least suitable. You must discuss your views as you cannot vote on the candidates.

You must also devise three questions you need to be answered for each candidate, so that you gain more specific information prior to the interview.

Your meeting will last for 30 minutes. If you fail to agree on the order, no one will be recruited and it will be six months before another shortlist will be compiled.

Good luck.

Candidate 1: Gerald Atkinson

Gerald has worked in a number of different industries during his career. He has been working successfully for four years as an area manager for a double-glazing company. He has a team of six salesmen who are responsible for selling £20,000 worth of product each month. He trains and coaches each person in the art of selling.

He enjoys his current job and regularly exceeds the budget target for the area. This has been recognized by various sales awards over the last few years.

He has previous experience in the brewing trade where he was an area manager responsible for a team of six salesmen. This is a job he performed for eight years, regularly exceeding the sales budgets for his area. He likes working in the industry and still has a number of active contacts.

He has no formal qualifications but has regularly attended training courses in topics for sales, marketing and people management. He has tried to put these into action as much as possible.

Away from work, Gerald is active in the Terrence Higgins Trust. He is involved as the local chairman and has on occasion appeared on television to represent the charity. He plays football in the local Sunday league and has been leading scorer in his league four times in seven years.

Candidate 2: Kevin Ferguson

Kevin has worked for a major pub tenancy company as a regional manager for the past two years, looking after 22 tenanted pubs. He likes his work, especially the social contact with the tenants.

During his two years, he has been managed by his Area Director, who he sees every two weeks. This frequency is due to him being fairly new to the company and trade. He visits each tenancy at least once per month.

In his two years, he has achieved his budget figures and has built a good social relationship with each tenant except one. He enjoys the relationship with the tenants and feels they trust him, which makes his job more rewarding.

He is about to go on a marketing course as he has not been able in the past to help tenants with their marketing. He does not feel that this has hampered his efforts, as he has done his best to help.

In his spare time he is involved in local politics. This involves having been a local councillor for the past five years. This takes up at least two nights a week as well as the occasional Saturday. He does not mind this as he feels he is putting something back into the community.

Prior to working in the brewing trade, he was a retail assistant in Boots. He liked the work but prefers to get out of working in one place all of the time. He worked at Boots since leaving school, where he gained six O Levels.

Candidate 3: Warren Giggs

Warren is an experienced manager who has worked for the last three years as an area manager for a large retail chain. He is responsible for the profitability of 30 stores through the efforts of the stores' managers.

During his time as area manager he has grown the business by 3 per cent, which is in line with other similar retail outlets. He has been able to achieve a lot of changes in working practices. This has resulted in a high turnover of managers of 27 per cent.

His previous experience was 10 years as a road supervisor in a building company, and seven years in the army as a sergeant in the Catering Corps.

He has no formal qualifications, but feels he is able to cope with most situations using common sense. He regards himself as being active and enjoys contact with people. However, his current role means he visits each site once every two months.

He takes an active role in the local branch of Friends of the Earth and is currently the secretary. He is committed to the movement and has been involved in various protest marches and sit-ins. He has been arrested once in connection with this.

Candidate 4: Nicki Taylor

Nicki left college four years ago where she did a Master's degree in management. She received a special award for being the best student in her final year.

Since leaving college, she has worked with a large soft drinks company in the merchandising field. This has involved working with retail managers to increase their sales of cola. Her initial task was to increase sales in her area by 10 per cent, which she achieved within three months. Since then she has been given larger projects as well as a larger area. Her performance over the last six months has involved a 20 per cent increase in sales.

She is actively involved in customer relations and has a thorough grasp of the marketing concept. This has impressed her boss. Her main area of concern at work is her current lack of involvement in the financial side of the business. She feels she has a lot to learn but feels she could do it if given the opportunity.

In her private life she is living with someone who is involved in the temperance movement and is in the Salvation Army. She assists with a local child helpline in the evenings and at weekends.

She enjoys the company of a good book or TV show rather than going out to socialize.

This exercise has asked you to rank a number of candidates for a particular role. However, with this one there is also another requirement, in that you are asked to develop three questions for each candidate based on the information in the profiles. This is often overlooked by a group who get excited about the profiles. They try to cover their tracks by suggesting the same three questions to all candidates; this is always seen as a fudge as the brief requests specific questions for each candidate.

As with previous examples, this exercise should be run as a meeting and as such needs to be planned effectively. There is limited time, and you need to achieve the two objectives, so time needs to be allocated to each task. A criteria approach could be used, as well as a discussion of the facts. What is important is to keep to the facts and not stray into bias areas that are not relevant to the role. This could include outside interests which may seem positive but do not add to the applicant's ability to perform the role. You need a method or criteria to discuss the candidates against so that they are all handled effectively and correctly. Your role is to:

- ensure your views are heard;
- try to influence the group towards your views;
- involve others;
- listen to what is said;
- ensure time is being used effectively as well as keeping the discussion on track.

TRY THIS: Practise problem solving

Looking at the exercise above, try to determine three or four suitable criteria to measure each candidate against. You should then apply the criteria to the candidates to see how such an exercise works. Once completed, let a friend or colleague see your work and offer suitable feedback.

A common trick

You all go into an exercise believing you all have the same brief. It is only natural to think you are getting the same information as the others on the event. On occasions this will not be the case, and this can cause confusion. Let us look at such an exercise.

EXAMPLE COMPETITIVE BRIEF: Promotion

During this exercise you are playing the role of a department manager brought together with other department managers at short notice to make a group decision: which one of six candidates will your group recommend to be promoted to a supervisory position in the production department? This decision must be made within 30 minutes. Following this group decision, one member of your group must represent all of you and make a verbal recommendation to the assessor team of the candidate selected. This recommendation must not exceed five minutes.

Note that your material contains six data sheets of candidates to consider for the promotion. The data sheet on top is the candidate you are to sponsor, but by the end of the 30 minutes the group must have a single choice.

You have 10 minutes to prepare for this meeting.

As you can see from the brief, you are being asked to champion a specific person. If you get this brief, you will not know if everyone has been asked to champion a different person. Your preparation will differ in this case, as you need to develop good arguments for your champion. You also need to look at the other candidates, as you do not have to succeed in getting your person the recommendation for promotion – you just need to champion their case. If there is a much better person, it makes sense to select them.

A trap a lot of people fall into is to feel they have to succeed and will be measured on that success. This can make them behave rather aggressively and switch the team off. If you behave like this, it will ensure you are seen negatively by the observers, as you will not be demonstrating interpersonal skills, effective influencing or team-work. You can often spot that this type of brief is being employed, as you will note that one of the participants is being more difficult than in previous exercises. They will become too pushy and possibly dismissive of other people's arguments. One way to tackle this is to let them know that their behaviour is not helping the process. This will show you have noticed the behaviour and have attempted to tackle the issue.

TOP TIPS: Problem-solving theoretical tasks

1 Use any planning time effectively.

2 Try to ensure the group members all have the same brief.

3 State your views and listen to others.

4 Plan how to make the required decisions.

5 Consider the criteria approach to overcome bias.

Ethical dilemmas: Decision making

This is a type of exercise that has been used a lot in the past, and is sometimes called a balloon exercise. This is because a famous exercise asked candidates to discuss and agree who should be removed from a hot air balloon that would crash and kill everyone on board if you did not throw someone over the side. In essence, you will face a problem where you have to decide the order in which a group of people will be rescued. There is always a timescale to the exercise and a chance that all will die if you do not make a decision. Like all the exercises, read it carefully and underline what has to be achieved. There are always clear constraints on this type of exercise; make sure you know and understand what they are and ask clarifying questions if you do not understand.

I have heard some candidates complain that this is unethical as it is about life and death, and many of these exercises do make people feel uncomfortable. This is ultimately up to you, but it can be helpful to remember that there is usually a good reason for the company to include such a task. For example, maybe they are recruiting for a management role that will involve having decision-making responsibility over redundancies, firings, raises, and other life-impacting things for their employees. This may be why this kind of exercise is used, as choosing who to let go could be a very real ethical dilemma faced by the successful candidate.

Don't forget, though, that you are selecting the company to join as much as they are selecting you. If you don't like what is in the exercise or it feels strange, it may factor into your decision to join the company. If you come across an exercise like this and you're not sure of the relevance, or the ethics, why not ask about it at the interview stage?

TOP TIPS: Ethical dilemmas

1 Ensure you identify how many tasks need to be completed and the constraints.

2 Plan how to deliver the brief successfully.

3 Give your views and listen to others' views.

4 Discuss and agree any order by using a process or criteria.

5 Make up your own mind.

Follow-up exercises

You will usually think that once an exercise is completed, you will not see it again. This is a reasonable thought, but one that at times will not be true. You may be asked on occasion to repeat an exercise or improve on what has been done previously. These types of exercise will be used to follow up on a previous exercise, either individual or group. You may not always see this coming; at times it may seem like it was a last-minute addition. It won't be though; it will have been planned in order to further test more competencies.

Follow-up group exercise

This can be used when a group exercise has been completed already. The group can be tasked with completing the task again with one or more of a few variations:

- using a different method;
- faster;
- cheaper.

You may be given the opportunity to choose an option or it may be stipulated. Whichever option is used, you need to show you feel it can be done and you want to succeed. Use all your influencing skills to make sure the team are positive about the new task. As you may imagine, this can sometimes be a real challenge to a group who have delivered a successful outcome. They may feel that they have already done well and achieved the task. I have experience of teams that at times resent having to do it all again, but look at it this way – this approach is used to test your tenacity and creativity, as well as the initial competencies from the original exercise. If the team are resisting, you will be seen in a good light if you are can persuade them to be positive and make a bigger impact.

Where a group have failed in an exercise, they can often feel this is a form of punishment for getting it wrong. Of course, no exercise is ever a punishment, despite how it may feel; you should instead see this as second chance to get it right. Be positive, as this exercise would have been set for you even if you had succeeded the first time. The real key is to encourage the group to stop and plan how to improve, without getting straight into the practical aspect. This might be hard, as the group already have experience of the task. If you're given the opportunity to choose your variation, and you feel your group may be reluctant to spend time re-planning, trying another method will challenge the group more than trying the same method faster or cheaper.

The approach to the exercise should follow what you have read earlier. You need to plan against the timescale and then deliver the plan. Be prepared to re-plan again if necessary – remember, the observer is interested in the process and behaviours of the group rather than whether you succeed.

Follow-up individual exercise

This type can easily be deployed in an assessment centre. It will relate to an exercise where you made your own decisions earlier in the day or in the previous exercise, to be repeated in a group. As we have seen in the previous chapters, the original exercise can be about how to move the organization forward, a priority exercise or a business game, and the aim of the follow-up will be for a group to discuss and agree a solution. You will in effect be running a meeting that is similar to the approach in the theoretical problem-solving exercises described in this chapter; you can follow that approach to reach a final position that is agreed by all involved.

EXAMPLE BRIEF: Follow-up exercise

This morning your group presented six different business ideas.

You are now required to discuss, debate and agree to retain only one of these six ideas, which you believe to be the most likely to succeed.

You should then collaborate to produce a two-year implementation plan to launch the retained idea in as much detail as you feel is necessary.

You have 90 minutes to complete this task.

This example is based on work completed earlier by the group; it could be used to follow up on one of the examples in Chapter 5. From the previous task, each member of the group has their own ideas and plan that have been outlined already, and you will all be required to select the best idea to proceed further. It can be tempting to treat an exercise like this as a challenge to push your own idea, but while there may be some value in having thought of the best plan, the real aim of the exercise is to select the best idea. You can show good problem solving and judgement in this exercise and still not have your idea adopted. This is not a problem as you will have focused on the aim of the exercise, not entered into a battle of ideas. The meeting you have will need to be structured and may utilize the criteria approach to identify the better projects.

Like with the other type of follow-up or repeat exercise, there is a danger of lethargy in the group caused by a feeling of frustration or boredom from tackling the same task twice, so you may need to vitalize the group to get a good solution. To do this, you can use all the tactics from the other group exercises: you can offer a process and a plan to ensure everyone is involved, which will show that you have people skills as well as process skills.

In all of the exercises like this example, there is rarely only one answer; in most cases it is just a matter of opinion. To gain success you need to:

- make sure your opinion is heard by the group with a logical, well-constructed argument;
- always make the best use of the planning time;
- encourage the team to invest some of the exercise time in planning;
- put a shape or structure to the exercise;
- work towards a structured solution;
- be positive and upbeat.

So, if you leave an exercise thinking about what you should have done or would like to have done, don't panic. You may get an opportunity to either do the exercise again or face a similar type of exercise later in the process. This will allow you to show you have learned from a previous experience and applied that learning rapidly, something that is prized by most forward-thinking organizations.

If you do not get an opportunity to put the plan into action, ensure you remember the points for use at your next assessment event. You will tackle the problem or exercise with a new confidence and a desire to do much better. You could also raise at the interview examples of what you have learned from the assessment process. This will make the employer aware of your self-evaluation and determination to correct these areas should you encounter them again.

The assessment process is where a company will learn about your skills and behaviour by observing your performance. You should also be learning during this process by evaluating your performance on each exercise. Look at what you did well and identify what you need to do to improve. If you carry out this self-evaluation your performance can only improve, and at the next event you will present yourself as a better candidate in all the exercises. This will help your confidence and will make you more likely to succeed.

TOP TIPS: Follow-up exercises

1 Clarify what is different about the brief and key points before you start.

2 Be prepared to plan the task in a different way to your past experience.

3 Listen openly to others' views as they will probably be different to what you have thought of before.

4 State your views with confidence and show a can-do approach.

5 Review the output against the objective at the end.

6 Use the OPPOSE techniques where appropriate

Key points to remember

1 Consider other candidates' ideas as they may be better than yours.

2 Sell your ideas with confidence.

3 Use a criteria approach to decision making to ensure you are focused on what has to be achieved.

4 Reject any areas of bias that have no part in the decisions.

5 Be prepared for surprises and always take a positive approach to those surprises.

08
Psychometric tests

Not all organizations use psychometric tests as part of the assessment process, but it's good to be ready for them, as many companies do use them to get a fuller picture of the candidate. There are three broad categories of psychometric test used in assessment centres: a personality or working preference profile, an aptitude test, and an evaluation of your skill level. Some assessment processes may use all three types of test, while others may just use one; it is best to establish if any are being used before you attend so that you are aware of what you will be facing.

It's natural to feel nervous about these tests, especially if you have not come across them before, but in reality they do have a high level of reliability due to the extensive validation process that has been established to ensure the test is measuring what it claims to measure, including making sure that the test administrator is trained and qualified (often by the British Psychological Society) to be able to do so. Try to think of them as another way to ensure that you and the role are the best possible fit for each other. To reduce nerves from unfamiliarity, you can practise similar tests before the assessment. Some tests are available on the internet, others can be purchased, and there are many books and other products on specific testing types, containing many practice questions and answers. If you are at university, you could also contact your careers advisor or employability department, where they should have access to personality profiles for you to practise.

Let us look at the three different types of test to ensure we understand what they are trying to achieve and how we should perform to get the best out of the process.

Personality/working preference profile

There are a great number of these types of profile in existence. They identify your interests, values, motivation and working preferences, and they all have their own particular uses in the world of work. This chapter is not about suggesting that one test is better than another, but it will simply outline what the profile measures and how it works. This in turn will aid you in completing the profile should it be used in one of your assessment events.

General rules

The first rule for all of these tests is: always read the instructions! It seems obvious, but it's easy to let nerves get ahead of you and not read them carefully. The instructions and scoring method will vary by test; in some instances you will use a number to score your answer and in others a set of letters to indicate your preferred answer. Take the time to read the instructions through and be clear what the score system requires at the start so that you do not make any mistakes.

Sometimes you will be required to complete the profile during the assessment event. You will be given a time target for this task, to encourage you to go with your natural instincts and not overthink the questions. Your instincts give a more accurate insight into your personality, so don't worry about getting the 'right' answer. However, in more recent times organizations have issued the profile to be completed online in advance, meaning the results are available to them prior to the assessment process, allowing more time for practical exercises on the day. Still, for this kind of test it's not about the 'right' answer, so you should go with your instincts anyway, as if you did have a strict time limit.

There will be times when you feel you cannot answer a question and want to come back to it later. Make sure you leave a gap in the answer sheet that relates to the question so that you do not put your next answers in the missing question box. This is a common error and can lead to strange results, not to mention causing panic when you get to the end and find you have one box still to fill. It is useful to make a mark on the question you intend to return to, which saves time in searching when you complete the profile and will also help if you fall into the trap just mentioned above.

Most profiles ask you to try to avoid the middle answer as much as possible. This is to ensure there is a clearer view of you; the middle option would lead to a bland and not very expansive picture of your personality or working style. However, you should use this option where you are unsure of the answer or it really is your preferred option.

With all personality profiles it is best to be as honest as you can be. Don't try to second guess what the organization is trying to measure. Most of these profiles have a consistency measure whereby they can see if you are trying to fake the result, so you likely won't get away with it. More importantly, the profile results if you try to 'game the system' will not be the genuine you, so it will not give you any future benefit as the organization may not be the best fit for you.

The results of personality or working-style profiles will be used to assist the interview process, and to help identify training and development needs for the successful candidate or candidates.

OPQ (Occupational Personality Questionnaire)

This is a British profile that has been in existence for over 30 years. Produced by the SHL group (Saville et al, 1994, 2007), who have extensive profiles across many areas, it is the most commonly used profile in the UK. It consists of a series of statements against which you have to rate yourself using a numerical scale from 1 (strongly disagree) to 5 (strongly agree). You are encouraged to stay away from the middle (3 – unsure) option. (See Figure 8.1.)

Figure 8.1   Typical question in the style of OPQ

I tend to talk too much

Strongly disagree	Disagree	Unsure	Agree	Strongly agree
1	2	3	4	5

The profile usually takes around 40 minutes to complete, but has no time limit. There are a number of versions available, but the most used is version 5.2 which has 248 statements. It can be scored using either a general population norm or a management and professional norm, meaning your outcome can be looked at against people in similar types of role to the one you are testing for. There are 30 different areas scored, broken down into three main sections, namely: relationships with people, thinking style, and feelings and emotions. You will get either a low, high, or medium score on each of the 30 areas, where a low score indicates that this area is not a key strength. Be aware, though, that having a high score is not always good. For example, there is an area related to worrying when things go wrong, and a high score here may show that you worry too much for the role. In contrast, a high score on the area of forward planning may be essential for the role.

As mentioned above, my advice here is to be honest; by trying to guess what is required you will make a mess of the profile and it will clearly not correctly represent you as an individual. Your results will show some of the strengths you think are important, but will inevitably also show some low areas which in reality are strengths for you. By being honest, the organization get to see the real you – which is the one they will employ.

The Cattell 16PF (16 Personality Factors)

This is a well-established personality profile which is used more than any other profile across the world (Cattell, 2003). It was established before the OPQ and took over two decades to develop. It sets out to measure 16 personality factors (as the name implies), as well as five global factors or themes (see Figure 8.2).

Figure 8.2 Five global factors (16PF)

Extraversion	Introversion
Independence	Accountability
Tough minded	Receptive
Self-control	Unrestrained
Low anxiety	High anxiety

You are required to respond to 185 statements using one of three options: A (yes it applies to me), B (it sometimes applies to me) or C (no it does not apply to me). As with the OPQ test, there are also consistency scores to identify if the person is completing the process in a truthful manner. (See Figure 8.3.)

Figure 8.3   Typical layout of a 16PF question

Do you like talking to new people?

A	B	C
Yes	Sometimes	No

This is an example of the format and is not part of the 16PF questionnaire.

There are other versions of this profile that are quicker to complete, such as 16PF 5, the use of which is becoming more commonplace. The output of the profile can also be compared with similar professions or jobs. This helps to identify trends and useful characteristics that will aid the settling-in process in a particular role.

Belbin team profile

This is a well-researched British profile that looks at your preferred role in a team (Belbin, 1981). It has been utilized by many organizations when faced with putting a project team together, and also by established teams to help them work even better together. It is a practical tool that will give you some good information about how you like to work in teams, as opposed to a straightforward personality profile.

The profile offers nine team roles, which are identified using a questionnaire designed around statements that relate to a work situation. Below each statement are a number of sentences about ways you may work. You are required to allocate 10 points on each sheet against the work sentences, choosing up to three sentences to allocate your points. You give your highest score to the sentence that best suits the way you work – so if only one sentence on the sheet fits you, this sentence will get all 10 points. If you choose two or three sentences you have to allocate the points to each sentence in line with your preference. You could offer eight points to one sentence and one point each to the other two, or you could select the points as five, three, and two – or whatever split (of whole numbers only, no fractions) fits your choice. This may sound complicated, but it is easy to get the hang of. Do check, though, that each statement has a total of 10 points allocated against the sentences; you will be surprised how often a mistake is made.

The outcome from this profile will be that you have identified the preferred role and secondary role for when you work in a team. The profile will offer a number of strengths and allowed weakness to be considered. Most people will be able to see how this works for them, and it has high reliability amongst those who have used it at work. Over time you may develop your skills and your team roles may alter. So, if you have completed this profile in the past, don't attempt to think about your previous answers, but answer the questions as you see them today.

Myers–Briggs Type Indicator (MBTI)

This is a well-established personality profile that was developed in the United States, although it also has a European English version (Briggs Myers, 2000). The two developers – Katharine C. Briggs and Isabel Briggs Myers – spent over 40 years developing this most useful tool for use in identifying your preferred style and method of interacting with others.

This profile works on the basis of a spectrum in four areas. In each of these four areas, the profile will show you your preferred end of the spectrum, which is expressed as a four-letter representation of your preferred method of working with others. There are 16 potential results for this profile, each 'type' showing how you view the world and interact with other personality types, along with your potential strengths and improvements that could be made. I have seen this profile used to excellent effect; when used with an existing team, the results and understanding from just four letters can be amazing. (See Figure 8.4.)

This profile can be completed online as well as at the assessment event. It has a self-score version as well as one that is scored by the

Figure 8.4   MBTI four types

Source of energy	
Extrovert	Introvert
Taking in information	
Sensing	Intuition
Decision making	
Thinking	Feeling
Lifestyle	
Judging	Perceiving

assessor, but they are all the same as they give the same result. You should expect two parts to this questionnaire. The first is about how you 'usually act or feel', with only two options for the answer, and you have to choose the answer that is nearest to how you act or feel. The second area consists of pairings of two words, where you have to identify which of the two words 'appeals to you more'.

Aptitude tests

These are often used to identify how a person will react to a certain type of work, for example problem solving with engineering diagrams or circuits, or applications to IT systems. There are many in existence that have a high reliability and can assist in predicting if a person will be able to perform tasks that are relevant to a particular role. Aptitude tests are usually carried out under exam-type conditions against a time limit, and they have all been developed and validated over many years to ensure they deliver what is required. Some common industries where you can expect to encounter them include engineering, computer programming and air traffic control – although any industry or company may use them.

Most of these exercises comprise diagrams or numbers. You will be asked to identify which of a number of options would either be the correct option to solve a problem or would be the next step in a process. As you will gather, these are not simple exercises or straightforward numeracy tests (we will look at those next) but are more complex and designed to replicate the skill required for a particular role.

You can usually expect a test of this type to last for between 15 and 30 minutes. You will be given an answer sheet to complete, most of which will have a sample section before you start, in order to prepare you for the type of questions you will face. Always take these sample questions very seriously, and take your time going through them, as they are a good guide to what you have to do in the real test. You will also get the answers to these sample questions from the person who administers the test. If you do not understand the question or do not understand the answer, always say so at this stage. The administrator will give you the correct answer, which may help you work out where you have gone wrong. If you are still stuck, ask the administrator for assistance in understanding the question. They will not start the test until everyone is ready and understands what they have to do.

As with all the other tests mentioned in this chapter, it is important to read or listen to the instructions carefully and pay attention to the answer sheet – don't let an avoidable mistake throw you off! You may feel pressure, with aptitude-type tests, to complete all the questions, but this is not actually something to worry too much about, as this is not how the tests are usually scored. Instead, your answers are compared against the correct answers a typical group would score. This means that you can still score highly when you complete only around three-quarters of the questions.

The most important thing to remember is that these tests are about your aptitude to do a particular task. If you get a low score, this may be an area where you have low aptitude at the moment, but it does not mean that you do not have other valuable strengths. It may sound obvious, but it can be hard to remember in the moment that tests such as these should be seen as an indicator of how well a task and a person are suited to each other, not as an indicator of you as a person. It cannot, of course, test your value!

Skills tests

This type of test is in common use in the UK and across the globe. Unlike the aptitude tests, which can be complex and specific, a skills test is where you may be tested for your ability to work with a more general skill, such as numbers or interpreting data, and they are incredibly common in recruitment and assessment processes. Many people will find this type of test relates to similar approaches they have experienced at school, so depending on your school experiences, you will either find these familiar and comfortable – maybe even like them! – or have some reservations. If the latter is true for you, it is best to put your past experiences out of your mind and look at these as a new challenge. The good thing about these tests is that, unlike personality profiles, each question will almost certainly have one correct answer – that kind of logical certainty can be comforting in an uncertain situation like an assessment centre!

Before starting one of these tests, it is fairly common practice that just like in the other kinds of tests you will see a number of sample questions. These give you the feel for what will follow and allow you to get comfortable with the format; they are not part of the test, so if you make mistakes it will not count against your score. There is usually no time limit on these sample questions, so take your time to ensure you fully understand the question. Again, it's important that if you don't understand the question or the answer, be vocal with your problem. Part of the administrator's role is to ensure that you do not start the exercise until you have become comfortable with the sample answers.

When you move on to the main body of the test you will be made aware of how long it will last and how to record your answers. These tests usually last from 20 to 30 minutes, and in that time you will be required to answer 30 to 40 questions. This will seem a lot but once you commence you will be able to move quickly through the process. Like with aptitude tests, you may feel you should answer all the questions in the time allocated, but it is best to try to get the answers right rather than rush to finish – you are not scored as a percentage, but rather against similar groups of people who have done the same test. Just like with aptitude tests, you can score very highly on three-quarters of the questions if they are correct. Remember, it is very likely that if you have struggled to complete the test in the time limit, so will others. A tip I have found helpful is to use the last 10 seconds of the test to fill out the remaining blank questions with any answer so that they have a chance of being correct. The idea is to score the last few missing questions with the same answer, for example, just picking the first answer for all of them, because in this way, if there are three options, you have a one-in-three chance of getting an answer right. There is rarely a score for getting answers wrong, so you will probably get a few more marks – it is a risk, but a calculated one!

Numeracy tests

When answering questions based on numeracy, you can use spare paper to calculate the answer. In some cases you will be allowed to use a calculator, so you should bring one along if you might be sitting a numeracy test, but do be aware that in other tests they want to see your knowledge and skill, so the calculator will not be allowed.

TYPICAL NUMERACY QUESTIONS

Below are examples that are not from any existing tests.

1: If a business has sales of £30,000 per month, what will be the annual sales?

Answer 1: £300,000
Answer 2: £400,000
Answer 3: £360,000
Answer 4: £420,000
Answer 5: Cannot say

2: If a person takes three weeks to complete a task working on their own. How many similar tasks would they complete in 10.5 weeks?

Answer 1: 3
Answer 2: 5
Answer 3: 3.5
Answer 4: 4.5
Answer 5: Cannot say

As you can see, you need to be able to look at data and how it is used. In the examples above, the answer to both questions is 3. In the first question, it is a matter of multiplying the monthly sales by 12, the number of months in a year. In question two it is a matter of dividing the 10.5 weeks by the time of one task (three weeks). This gives the answer of 3.5 tasks. The 'cannot say' option is used where the data does not have enough information to be able to draw a reasonable conclusion. Don't be afraid to use this option, but always ensure first that the other options are not correct.

On some tests you will be given graphs and charts to interpret your answer. The data will be fairly easy to read and understand once you have become familiar with the content. You need to be able to find data on the graph or chart and make good sense of its relevance. Be clear before you start about the type of data that is available from each graph or chart. From time to time you may have no relevant data about a question, so your answer may well be 'cannot say'. Check the charts before you use this option to ensure there is no relevant data. Where such data is used, you will still have practice questions before the test starts, containing graphs and charts so that you become familiar with their use. The purpose of the sample questions is to help you use the charts, but it is usual that in the real test you will be faced with a different set of graphs or charts, so don't be surprised when this happens.

Comprehension tests

For this sort of test, you will usually be given a piece of text containing information, and will be asked various questions about the content. They are usually multiple choice and are used to establish if you can look at a text and interpret correctly what is being said.

EXAMPLE: Comprehension questions

Please read the information below and answer the three questions that follow.

The game of rugby union in the UK has grown steadily in popularity over the past 10 years. There are now more people watching the game than at any other period of time. This is in part due to the coverage on TV as well as the success of the national teams at the Rugby World Cup, especially the British and Irish Lions. The female game has gathered pace since the English team won the World Cup in 2014.

Sponsorship for the game has been increasing at a national level. However, local teams have struggled more than before to get sponsorship at a level that will allow them to grow even more.

Q1: There is a greater interest in rugby union than in the past.

Answer 1. True
Answer 2. False
Answer 3. Cannot say from the information provided

Q2: The female game of rugby union is now more popular than the male game.

Answer 1. True
Answer 2. False
Answer 3. Cannot say from the information provided

Q3: Local rugby clubs are finding it easier to get sponsorship than in the past

Answer 1. True
Answer 2. False
Answer 3. Cannot say from the information provided

The biggest thing to watch out for on this type of test is to never make assumptions or draw conclusions, as the text will only show facts. From the text, you will see that for the first statement, answer 1 is correct, as the text clearly states that there is a greater interest in rugby union than before. The second statement asks about an area to which the text does not actually refer, although it seems to – it talks about the female game of rugby union but does not actually compare it to the male game, which is what the statement says. Therefore, the answer has to be option 3, 'cannot say from the information provided'. Finally, the third statement is false, as the text clearly states that at a local level it is more difficult, not easier, to obtain sponsors, so the correct answer is 2.

Only one part of the process

Do not be afraid about any tests or profiles you may be set. They are designed to help the recruitment process and enable a positive fit between the job role and the person. It will be extremely rare for an organization to base their selection decision on tests alone; they are one factor in a multi-factor approach. If you have difficulty with them, remember that others will face similar problems, and that you may have other strengths that far outweigh these results. Such tests may only show that you have a specific development requirement, and you cannot do any more than your best in this situation.

Key points to remember

1 Be honest with your answers in all personality profiles.

2 Do not try to skew any profile answers by writing what you feel the organization wants to see.

3 Always take the trial questions seriously and seek out the correct answer before you commence the test.

4 Practise tests and profiles if you get the opportunity.

5 You can still get a high score if you fail to complete a test.

References

Belbin, M (1981) *Management Teams: Why they succeed or fail,* Heinemann. Belbin website: www.Belbin.com

Briggs Myers (2000) *An Introduction to Type: A guide to understanding your results on the Myers–Briggs Type Indicator,* European English Version, Oxford Psychologists Press. Website: www.myersbriggs.org

Cattell, H (2003) *Essentials of 16PF Assessment* (Essentials of Psychological Assessment), Wiley. 16PF website: www.16pf.com

Saville, P et al (1994, 2007) Occupational Personality Questionnaire Concept Model, *BPS Review*. Website: www.SHL.com

09
The interview

Unlike a 'traditional' recruitment process, which relies on a series of interviews, in an assessment centre the interview will form only a small part of the overall mechanism. It will have a weighting like all the other parts of the process, but will not be used as a way of eliminating candidates from the running. They are normally used to give recruiters a more rounded view of you and give you the chance to talk about specific areas that may be of particular concern or interest to the employer. Because of this, you should look on the interview as an opportunity both to leave a very positive professional impression, and to talk about the areas of the role that may be of particular concern or interest to you. Remember, the interview is a two-way process, and as such is a chance for you to be active in ensuring the employer really learns about you and your skills, as well as allowing you to learn more about the role and company culture.

Not all assessment centres will use an interview on the actual day; however, if you are successful at the assessment stage you will inevitably face an interview before you get a job offer. The basic principles of the interview are the same whether it is part of the assessment event or is a follow-up activity.

How the employer prepares

As with the assessment centre process as a whole, by understanding how the employer prepares for the interview, and what they are usually looking for, you can better prepare for an outstanding performance. Most organizations will begin by reviewing the job description and person specification for the role, to identify what is important to the job and how it is performed. As we saw in Chapter 2, the job description will outline the key tasks of the job as well as the accountabilities and outputs that are required. The person specification outlines the skills, knowledge and personal attributes required to perform the job effectively, and is designed to go alongside the job description, although not every organization will use one. These attributes are usually broken down into essential (someone could not do the job without these) and desirable (characteristics that would help, or be nice to have, but which wouldn't prevent someone getting the job if they didn't have them); this list can be used to differentiate between two close candidates.

From these two documents, a series of questions are developed to test whether the person has the correct attributes. During the assessment process the observers have been looking for practical evidence to demonstrate these competencies, and the interview is to provide more evidence for this. If I ask you, 'Can you solve problems?', most people will naturally say yes – an answer that provides little or no information for the company, as they only have your word that you can do the task. The organization does not know how you go about solving problems or if you are any good at the task, therefore this is a very poor question to ask on its own. You are much more likely to be asked what are called competency questions; for example, if I asked you, 'Can you explain how you have solved a complex problem in the past?', I will get a lot more information. We will see what you did and how you did it. This gives a better view of you as a person and how you work.

How to prepare for the questions

If you can identify the competencies in advance of the interview, you can make a reasonably accurate attempt at guessing the questions you may face, and be able to prepare answers in advance that are relevant to the role and your skills.

Let us look at a typical job description for an Office Manager. From this we should try to identify the key tasks and competencies that are relevant to this role.

JOB DESCRIPTION: Office Manager

Location: Head Office.
Staff numbers reporting: 12 full-time staff.
Purpose of job:

- ensure the smooth running of Head Office administration;
- ensure all staff are able to perform their own duties (ie payroll) to the required standard;
- facilitate field staff in performing their role and provide necessary information in a timely manner.

Responsibilities:

- maintain staff at a performance level that achieves organization goals;
- recruit staff as required to maintain staff levels;
- maintain staff motivation at all times;
- comply with all relevant employment law in the UK;
- maintain knowledge of other areas of the business to ensure budgets are achieved and information correctly recorded;
- comply with all health and safety requirements for the organization;
- comply with all policies set out by the board to enhance business performance;
- set the limit of spending level for staff, ie admin assistant, and monitor the outputs;
- represent the organization at business functions;
- act as the first line in maintaining the discipline standards of the organization;
- develop the skills of staff in order to enhance the department's level of performance;
- recommend methods to improve the performance of the organization.

Line manager: Managing Director.
Key Contacts: Company Secretary and Financial Controller, all other staff in Head Office.

This is only half the story. We need to consider what the person specification will outline, although you may not get this piece of information as it can sometimes only be available for internal use by the organization. Nonetheless, let us look at how this could be set out for the role above.

PERSON SPECIFICATION: Office Manager

- Previous Office Manager experience in other companies;
- career history, full details of all companies;
- career aspirations – if any (do not want highly ambitious person);

Technical:

- looking for examples of further education;
- previous training or work experience;
- exposure to related areas – it/accounts/hr/monitoring;

Behavioural:

- attention to detail – data analysis;
- interpersonal sensitivity;
- planning and organizing;
- delegation;
- business awareness;
- flexibility.

Biographical:

- previous experience in Office Manager role;
- career history and reasons for leaving current post;
- hobbies and interests (team sports);
- further career aspirations (limited promotion facilities).

Technical:

- qualification in higher education;
- qualification relevant to post (ie diploma in office management).

Behavioural:

- planning and organizing;
- detail handling (filing);
- business awareness (data protection/employment law);
- interpersonal sensitivity (harmony within the office).

Once you have looked at this you should be able to see what the organization will be trying to identify in a job applicant. You may wish to try the exercise from Chapter 2 again. Before reading on, jot down on a spare piece of paper the attributes and skills you think the company is looking for based on the examples above.

Having done that, you should have been able to identify a number of key requirements for this role, and for all of these requirements, your interviewers will have to identify clear questions to test your skills and knowledge. (Remember, though, that not all attributes may feature in the interview, as some companies will decide that the other assessment activities will provide enough evidence without further questioning.)

Based on this example, the interviewers would be asking how you have demonstrated the following **competencies**:

- decision making;
- communication – written;
- communication – verbal;
- fact finding;
- analysis of data;
- task management;
- interpersonal skills.

Your interviewers would also want to explore how you have achieved some of the **tasks** outlined in the job description:

- motivated staff;
- developed and appraised staff;
- handled flexibility;
- negotiated with suppliers.

Having identified these things, the organization will then develop suitable questions to test all of the above, and you will need to identify how to answer these in an interview. Here is an example of how an organization might develop questions based on the competencies and tasks identified.

TYPICAL QUESTIONS FOR THE OFFICE MANAGER

Decision making:

- Describe how you made a decision about improvements within the office procedure and how did you implement it?
- How did you arrive at your decision?

  - advice of staff;
  - external advice.

Communication written – staff appraisals:

- What experience do you have of staff appraisals?
- Can you explain the format of the appraisal and describe what the appraisal involved?
- How did you record the relevant details of the conversation?
- What did you do with the results of the appraisal?
- What was the most significant achievement in your last job?
- How did you motivate staff in your last job?
- What reactions did you get to your approach?
- How did you deal with any negative responses?

Fact finding:

- Explain your involvement in the recruitment of staff in the past.
- What level of the decision were you involved in?
- Could you describe what factors would make you select an individual?
- What difficulties did you face with the recruitment?
- How did you overcome these difficulties?

Analysing data:

- Describe how you negotiated a price with an external supplier for goods or services.
  - How did you go about this?
  - Why was this important?
  - What was the result?
  - What would you do differently in the future?
- Can you give an example of how you use data to enhance the performance of your team?
  - What effect has this had on the people/business?

Effective communication (verbal/written):

- Explain how you have implemented a new piece of software or new process that affected several members of staff.
  - How well did they understand it?
  - What feedback did you receive?
  - What were the results?

Task management:

- Describe a situation when you had to produce work to a tight timescale.
  - Give me an example of how you changed the work of you and your team.
  - What problems did you encounter – how did you ensure these did not occur again?

- Explain how you have managed a budget successfully.
  - What was it?
  - How did you apply yourself to it and what tasks did you carry out?

Liaising with manager:

- Describe a situation when you needed to report a problem to your line manager.
  - How did you resolve the issue?

Flexibility:

- Describe a time when you needed to change your priorities.
  - How did you react?
  - What did you do to reorganize your existing workload?
  - What would you do differently?
- Explain how you have communicated a change in workload to your staff.
  - How did you organize the messages?
  - What participation did you expect from staff?
- Describe how you accomplished your most significant achievement in your last job.
  - Why was it significant?
  - What effect did it have on others?
  - What results did it have?
- Describe how you motivated your staff to achieve a difficult task.
  - How did they react?
  - How did you maintain motivation?
  - What results did they achieve?
  - What would you do differently?

As you can see, these are not simple yes or no questions, but require a lot of thought. You want to find the correct example to use, and know you are capable of answering any relevant follow-up questions. By identifying these in advance you can start to prepare ready-made and credible answers to potential questions.

TRY THIS: Competency examples

Look at the competencies identified from the examples above. For each of these, try to identify relevant examples of how you meet that competency. At this stage, do not worry about the answer to the question in too much detail, but try to have at least two relevant examples for each competency you may face. It's fine to use the same example in a few different competencies, as most people use a combination of competencies when performing any task. If you can't think of any examples from a work setting, you should also consider examples in your social life or school experience.

Table 9.1 Typical competency examples

Competency	Examples of achievement
Communication verbal	
Communication written	
Interpersonal skills	
Planning and organizing	
Fault finding	
Problem analysis	
Decision making	
Cash management	
Innovation	
Leadership	
Teamwork and motivation of team	
Customer focus	
Tenacity	
Drive	
Flexibility	
Integrity	
Business acumen	
Functional knowledge	

Answering questions

Once this is complete, you need to consider how best to answer questions about these areas. To do this successfully you need to have a process to follow that you can apply to any given question in the knowledge that you have covered all the required detail. One useful method I have found to help with competence-based questions is the SPARD method (sometimes called the STAR method). This is fairly simple to use and will allow you to both prepare in advance of the interview, and react to questions in the interview that you had not considered. SPARD is a pneumonic for:

- S – Situation;
- P – Problem;
- A – Action;
- R – Result;
- D – Different.

Each area is important and they should be used in this order. When a question requires you to talk about how you did a task or tackled a situation, you can employ the SPARD method. Explain the **Situation** you faced, giving any necessary background. You can then talk about the **Problem** you encountered and the **Actions** you decided to take, along with your thinking behind these actions. You are then able to talk about the **Result** of your endeavours and how you gained a positive outcome. Finally, you can talk about what you have learned from the experience that would make you act **Differently** in the future. This final area is not always requested, but it is useful as it shows that you are able to reflect on what has happened. (The STAR method functions in the same way – Situation, Task, Actions, Result – but I personally prefer SPARD because it includes that extra level of analysis and reflection at the end.)

Following this simple structure gives a fully rounded answer to what can feel like a difficult question. You have clear steps to take that will make you appear to be in control of the input and will show you to be an excellent communicator. The final area (different) will show that you are always open to learning experiences. The result is that you are seen as a good candidate who is confident and competent.

Here's an example in practice:

QUESTION AND SPARD ANSWER

What is the most difficult problem you have had to face?

Situation. I was the manager of a team of four people in an IT team. Our role was to provide assistance to all staff who were encountering IT or software problems. The team of four were all good at what they did and had a great reputation with the client base. I had a close relationship with the team based on three years of working together.

Problem. I was asked by my manager to reduce my team from four to two members as part of a company redundancy scheme where the company was reducing in size by 50 per cent. Selecting two of the team was difficult as they were all good at their role and none of them had caused any problems with their performance.

Action. I talked to each person in turn to make them aware that they were under threat of redundancy and all four stated they would prefer to remain with the company. Therefore, I had to make a decision about which two would be selected for redundancy. I developed a grid of skills for the job as all four had the same length of service and qualifications. The grid identified the range of work, the ability to complete tasks, customer reviews of service and complexity of their skills.

Result. When applying these areas it was clear that two individuals were good at what they could do but were limited in the range of tasks they could perform. These two also had more negative customer reviews than the other two IT professionals. This made the selection easier but still very hard to explain to the individuals. Whilst they could see the rationale for the decisions they were unhappy to leave the company. I remained firm with my decision and both left at the appropriate time.

Different. I learned a great lesson from this problem, which has helped me in the role ever since. I now regularly ensure that the skills of everyone in my team are more comprehensive than before. I review the skills and their application every three months to ensure that development has happened. I also share customer feedback with each individual and develop methods to enhance their service levels. This makes the team stronger and gives the customer a better service.

As you can see, this process is easy to follow and can be adapted to any question. A good tip to really get the most out of this method is to focus on what you did to address the issue. Focus on your role and actions and be positive about the result; you should be talking about 'I' not 'We' unless it is about teamwork, and even then you should talk about what you did to enhance the team.

TRY THIS: Practice SPARD exercise

Using the list of competencies and tasks identified in the earlier examples, pick another one (or two) and use the SPARD method to develop your answer.

Use the grid below to make notes.

Table 9.2   Sample answers

Situation
Problem
Action
Result
Different

Once you have your answer planned out, try to find someone to listen to it out loud to ensure it has a clear flow that will impress the interviewer. The more practice you do, the more ease and confidence you will have, and the better you will appear at the interview.

Asking questions

Now that you have a good idea of what questions the interviewer is likely to ask you, and you have planned and practised your answer, you should start to think about the job and identify if there are issues you need to discuss with the employer. For example, the job description goes only so far as to outline duties; you may need to discuss how the job operates and look at the environment. It is useful to list the questions you feel need to be addressed in order for you to decide if this is a role you want to perform. Some of these questions will have occurred to you from your earlier stages of preparation, but you may also wish to look at these four areas when thinking about what you need to know:

- organization;
- job role;
- colleagues;
- environment.

As we discussed in Chapter 4, you want to be aware of the impression you are giving when deciding which questions to ask. For this reason, try to focus more on the job than the conditions and payment at this stage, as these can be dealt with later – usually at the offer stage. At interview, you need to create an impression that you are the right person for the role and you want the job – interested, not desperate – and for better or worse, many employers still believe that asking about pay and benefits at this early stage gives an impression of being only focused on money, instead of interested in the job itself.

Here are some suggestions for questions you may wish to ask.

EXAMPLES OF QUESTIONS

1 Can you explain more about the day-to-day operations of the role?

2 Can you tell me about the challenges the role will face over the next 12 months?

3 Can you explain a typical progression route for this role within the company?

4 How will you measure my impact in the first three months in the role?

5 How do you live the values of the company?

6 How would you describe the culture of the company?

7 What changes will we see in the company over the next three years?

8 Where will the company seek to grow in the next three years?

9 How will my colleagues support new people coming into the organization?

10 How will you know I have gelled with my colleagues?

This is not a complete list, and not all of them will be appropriate for your particular situation; you, most importantly, need to consider what you need to know. However, the questions on this list cover a lot of positive ground and give the impression of someone who is forward-facing and company-focused.

TRY THIS: What do you want to know?

Using the example job in this chapter (or another job you are applying for), think about the things you would want to know to find out if it's the right job for you. Use the grid below to make some notes of questions in the different areas.

Table 9.3 Your questions

Organization
Job role
Colleagues
Working environment

A final note on preparation: having gone through all of the stages above, you have now done a lot of relevant work. You can enhance your chances of a successful interview even more by taking your notes and preparation documents with you to the interview, to refer to if you get stuck on a question that you have prepared in advance. All you need to do is look at the SPARD examples you have developed. You can also refer to your notes about the questions you have about the organization and the job. This will look natural and show you have taken the interview seriously by the amount of preparation you have done.

The interview process

You have prepared well for the interview. You have identified the competencies and skills the employer will require, practised using your answers to the typical questions you may face, and you have your thorough notes with you to prompt you on the day. What you now have to do is impress upon the interviewer that you are a credible candidate who can deliver success in the vacant role. The good news is you are already part way there – because you have prepared well!

The employer will use the interview for three main purposes:

- assess the candidate;
- explain the job;
- sell the organization.

You will be actively involved in the assessment as it is you they are assessing. You will have some prepared questions about the job that require clarification, so you are also involved in this aspect of the interview. As well as this, the employer will be selling the organization to you throughout the process. They want you to actively want to work for them, and they also hope you will talk positively to others about your experience with the recruitment process, so don't be surprised if they seem to be selling the positive aspects of the job. More importantly, those involved in the process will be trying to promote the organization by their positive approach and actions.

The arrangements

If the interview is integrated into the assessment day or days, you will already know where to be and when. If it's a separate interview, you will again be told in advance the time and date of the interview, and the venue – you may also be told the name of the interviewer in advance. This will help you, as you may have seen them before in one of the exercises, and you can be more relaxed with a known person than with a stranger. Just as with the assessment centre overall, you have to ensure you get there on time to maintain that first good impression; have another look at Chapter 4 to remind yourself of how to effectively prepare for this.

The room being used will be private, to ensure you can talk freely without other parties listening, and free of interruptions so that you have the total attention of the interviewer. The door may have a notice saying 'Do not interrupt' or 'Interview in progress'. When you see this, you will know the interviewers have taken their role seriously and professionally, and have thought about you and the positive impression they want to create. If there is more than one interviewer, you will probably find them behind a desk, with a chair across and nearby for you, to make conversation easy. Or there may be no desk and two or three people sitting together in a circle. If the organization has a lack of space you could find yourself in a room with a large table (boardroom style), in which case, you and the interviewer will likely be at one end close to each other. The worst situation is where the interviewer makes no attempt to create a rapport and sits directly opposite you across a big table. In this situation you can use your body language to help create that rapport – for example, mirror the interviewer's pose and body language, or lean slightly forward.

The format and what you should do

Most interviews have three main stages to ensure all issues are covered effectively:

- opening;
- information gathering;
- closing.

Opening

The opening is very important, as this is where you get to make a positive and lasting impression on your interviewers. This stage will usually last only three to five minutes, and you will be introduced to the interviewers, who will take the lead and explain what will happen during the interview. This will vary from company to company, but some things you might expect to hear are:

- that the interviewers will be taking notes to aid their memory of your answers;
- that the interviewers will take turns asking questions, or that one person may not ask any because they are focusing on listening;
- they may state the objective of the interview, ie to gather relevant information from you in order to make a quality decision about your suitability for the role;
- they should explain that you can ask questions about the role – usually at the end.

The main aim of this stage for the interviewers is to relax you so that you can think and talk freely about your skills and knowledge, and how they apply to the job role. The key things for you, the candidate, to consider are:

- believe that this is a two-way process;
- remember that you select the employer and they select you;
- you have an active part to play in the process.

By thinking this way you should relax into the conversation as you remember that you are also assessing the organization.

When entering the room make sure you:

- have a smile on your face; everyone likes a smile;
- look at the people in the room and move towards them;
- shake hands with the interviewers and introduce yourself;
- the handshake should be firm and not last too long.

The interviewers will introduce themselves and in order to recall the names you can repeat them back, for example, 'nice to meet you John and Sarah'. This helps create rapport and will make you sound confident.

Once you have entered the room you need to:

- have an upright posture to show confidence;
- sit in the chair provided but remain upright;
- keep your hands apart or on your preparation documents;
- try not to fold your arms, as this can be seen as defensive and will possibly show a lack of confidence;
- whilst the other party is talking ensure you look interested in what they are saying; you can do this by tilting your head slightly to the side and nodding when appropriate.

These techniques are used on TV by anyone interviewing a member of the public or a politician. Go and look at a news programme tonight to see this in action.

If you are asked any questions, make sure your voice is positive and modulated on key words. When people talk in a monotone voice, the other party tends to switch off and miss the points being made. You should use this approach throughout the interview.

Information gathering

The main body of the interview is where the information gathering takes place. This is where the interviewers will:

- ask their relevant questions about you, your abilities and history;
- take a lot of notes of what you say;
- listen intently to your answers;
- possibly summarize what you have said about a topic.

If they summarize, don't worry – it's not a trap, it's to ensure they have fully understood what you have said. You should agree with the summary and add any key information you feel they have missed. This is your chance to shine, with all your carefully practised SPARD examples! This stage – incorporating their questions and yours – will usually last around 50 minutes of an hour-long interview, and will involve you doing most of the talking.

As in the opening stage, your body language for this part of the interview is very important. Make sure you are demonstrating 'active listening':

- sitting upright in your chair (as opposed to slouching);
- using open hand gestures as you talk;
- making eye contact with the interviewers – ideally all of the panel, instead of focusing only on the person who asked you the question;
- summarizing back to the person what they have just said, to check and demonstrate that you understand.

This isn't everything, of course, and you shouldn't focus on appearing to listen more than you actually focus on listening, but this kind of body language is definitely a sign of an engaged and interested candidate.

At some stage, you will probably be asked for your views on the assessment process. This may be in one of two formats: first, how effective you thought the process was, and second, how you think you performed. This can be tricky to answer depending on your experiences and how you feel you performed, so always try to be positive about the process, but also honest. If you have any complaints, ensure you have a suggestion for improvement. This will help the organization and demonstrate your analysis of the situation.

If asked about your performance, you have an opportunity to demonstrate that you have considered what happened and have some key learnings to take forward. You can relate any difficult areas you encountered to a potential training solution, which shows you can be critically reflective of your own performance. It also demonstrates that you know how to improve in the future as you have reflected on the activities. This will be seen as a positive. Finally, you can explain your thoughts about why certain exercises did not go to plan. By explaining your ideas you may clear up any uncertainty in the minds of the assessors.

Anyone who moans about the process will not be taken seriously as they have not offered a solution to the problems they see. It sounds like they are blaming the process rather than owning their own performance, and most organizations will not welcome such people into their working environment.

In my experience it is not unusual for the organization to ask what you know about them, to see if you have researched the company you claim you want to work for. We looked in Chapter 2 at the kind of research to do, and this is where that, and your notes, will come in really handy. Always sound positive about what you have found, and try to use the most recent information first. You can outline the products and services as well as performance. Make the panel aware that you want to work for a company that is developing as much as this one.

This will be a good time to ask appropriate questions about the organization. You could say, 'I like what I have found out about the organization. I also have a few questions that will help clarify where the organization is going and assist my knowledge.' You can then ask a few questions. Again, listen intently to the answers and tilt your head to ensure it looks like you are listening. If appropriate, you can summarize what has been said to show that you have listened.

Towards the end of the interview, you will have the opportunity to ask your questions. You can decide how many to ask based on the description of the job so far, and the information they have given you. If it was well covered you may only have a few questions, but make sure you have listened, and take a moment to think again about your prepared list of questions. If some of them have already been answered, don't ask them again, as this will show that you haven't been properly listening – although it is worth saying that you had some questions about X but these have now been answered during the interview, as this shows you have prepared. You can now ask the questions that have not been covered so far, or any new questions that may have occurred to you during the main body of the interview.

The closing

The final stage, then, is the closing. This may be short, but don't switch off yet, as it will still give you relevant information. For example, the organization may summarize what has occurred and ask for any final questions or something you would like to add. You will be told the details of the next stage of the process and when you will be contacted (if you're not told this – ask!). Finally, the interviewers will thank you for your time and efforts during the interview. Maintain the positive, engaged body language that you have shown throughout the interview; when saying goodbye, thank the panel for their time, shake hands, use their names and make eye contact. Depending on what has been said, you could also say something like, 'I look forward to hearing from you' to indicate that you are still interested in the role.

Obviously, the details of this process will vary slightly from organization to organization, but the format that we have covered here is a fairly standard one, with features common across all interviews. Table 9.4 sums up the main points.

Table 9.4 Creating a positive impression

Interview stage	Interviewer actions and goals	Your key points and actions
Opening	Welcome you Introduce themselves and aim of the interview Explain the process	Positive body language – smile, firm handshake, eye contact Repeat names back (this will help you remember) Settle yourself, retrieve notes and water, and listen actively to process instructions
Information gathering (main body)	Asking questions Checking understanding of your answers, or asking for more detail Answer your questions	Answer questions using SPARD Open, active body language – eye contact, hand gestures, smile Active listening Ask prepared questions
Closing	Summarize next steps Thanks to you for your time and interest	Ask any final questions Affirm continued interest in opportunity Handshake and thanking by name

TRY THIS: Additional SPARD practice

If you would like to practise answering more questions, here are a few more that will help you use the SPARD approach. Although this list obviously doesn't cover all the questions you might face, it will help you to think about the kind of questions you could be asked.

Practice questions

1   Can you give me an example of how you usually achieve a goal?
2   Describe how you explained a complex situation to someone.
3   Explain how you have changed the way another person works.
4   How do you encourage other colleagues to reach or exceed the agreed work standard?
5   Describe a situation where you have brought a benefit to a working team.
6   What do you need from others at work to ensure you work effectively and achieve your goals?
7   Describe the most complex information you had to analyse.
8   Tell me about a situation where you have not trusted someone at work.
9   Describe the most difficult decision you have made.
10 Describe a situation where you had to change your priorities.

Key points to remember

1   Prepare for competence-based questions.
2   Use the SPARD technique to answer questions.
3   Ensure you look and sound positive with your body language.
4   Keep good eye contact with the interviewers.
5   Have a selection of relevant questions to ask at the end.

10

Dealing with difficulties and how to perform on the day

In previous chapters we looked at how to prepare for the assessment process and tackle each of the exercises you may encounter. We also covered the interview process and developed an approach to predicting and answering questions in a positive manner. We now need to consider how you will create – and maintain – a good first impression with the assessors and behave in an effective manner throughout the day itself. Although most of your preparation will focus on what you say and do, how you say and do it is also important. It is very easy to just say 'do your best', but what exactly does your best look like? In this chapter we will look at a positive strategy to deliver what is required by the organization and to represent yourself effectively; first, what to do in general that will present you in a positive light, and then various actions to take when you face different or unexpected problems. It is better to prepare for these in advance rather than attempt to find a solution when you are under the pressure of the event.

Polite and positive

This may seem obvious, but it always pays to be polite! During a pressured event such as an assessment day, it can be tempting to focus exclusively on remembering your preparation, showing off your skills to the assessors, and possibly even venting your stress when it seems like no decision makers are watching. However, all the people you meet on the day – from the receptionist and person serving coffee, to the other candidates and the silent observers – will form an opinion of you, and this opinion may be shared at some stage.

An example: I was part of an assessment team for a major hotel group who were recruiting potential managers from graduates in hospitality. It was a two-day event and included an evening meal attended by assessors, hotel managers and the previous year's graduates, as well as the candidates. Alcohol was available, and the focus was social interaction – it was a fun, relaxed part of the event. After the meal, the assessors and managers – the 'important' people – left the current graduates to socialize with the assessment candidates. The atmosphere was relaxed and social, and the candidates believed that everything they said was 'off the record'; however, the current graduates actually had a specific brief to find out if any of the candidates had already accepted a job with another hotel group. The next morning we were able to use the information from the current graduates to determine who to spend significant time with as a serious candidate, while those who were only along for the experience received a quicker interview. You are never 'off duty' in an assessment centre!

So, then, it is important to be actively positive and polite throughout the event. Your first point of contact will probably be with the receptionist or security team, and it can be too easy to think they are not part of the process. However, their views on candidates are often sought, and if you have been rude or unfriendly, that is what they will report. I have seen many a potential candidate be rude to a receptionist for no reason; it has never helped their recruitment and on occasions it has hindered their progress. You can never be sure if you are being observed outside of the exercises. Therefore, always stay positive and polite to everyone you meet, and don't let stress – or excessive alcohol at a seemingly 'off duty' social time! – negatively affect your behaviour.

TOP TIPS: Polite and positive

- Always be polite to the people you meet.
- Smile and look confident.
- Be positive about the job to everyone.
- Remember you are never off duty.

Arrival

In Chapter 4 we looked at planning your arrival so as to start off on the right foot. You will have arrived ahead of time, unrushed and feeling confident. You will have made a good impression with the reception staff or security, and are now being asked to come along to the venue where the exercises will take place.

At this stage you will meet the host and the assessors as well as some of the other candidates who will take part in the process. You're already aware of being polite and positive, so an appropriate greeting and saying who you are will be a great start. Couple this with a smile, an upright body posture and open gestures and you will have made a great first impression. However, there's likely to be some hanging around, and it can be very tempting to sit and look at your mobile phone or tablet while you are waiting to start. Perhaps you are feeling awkward, nervous or shy, but consider the impression this will make on the people who see you. Keeping to yourself will not allow you to show any of your interpersonal skills, or to get comfortable and confident with the other participants. My advice is to put the phone away and switch it off or onto airplane mode (not on silent or vibrate – it's best just to remove the temptation or possibility of distraction altogether). This will help you to be in the moment and to concentrate on your main task – being successful in the assessment process.

Turning your phone off now, before the start, will also allow you to take the opportunity to talk to some of your fellow candidates.

Smile, chat with others to help put yourself more at ease; talk positively about the event and seek out their views on what they believe will happen during the course of the event. Who knows, they may share a useful insight you have not considered. At worst they could be wrong, but you have had time to consider how you would react to what they have suggested, and by talking to the others in the group you are creating a better atmosphere, which will help you feel confident and comfortable and perform at your best. Remember, too, that you are never off duty, and by actively engaging with the other candidates, the assessor will see you as a person with confidence and good interpersonal skills.

Before the event begins properly, the leader or host will most likely give a welcoming talk to outline what will happen, and give time to address any issues the group may have before beginning. Practical considerations such as the room layout and other additional rooms will be explained, as well as a timetable of the event. Listen carefully to anything they say at this stage to confirm your preparation and help you to stay relaxed.

TOP TIPS: Arrival

- Be on time.
- Switch off your phone.
- Talk to the other candidates.
- Be friendly and smile.
- Act confidently.

Exercises

When any exercise is given to you or a group, always smile and stay positive. Look like you are welcoming the challenge, even if you are tired or have faced a similar task before. Such an approach makes you look positive in the eyes of the assessors and that is who you are trying to impress.

Remember the basics of any exercise you are given, which are to listen carefully to what is said, take any relevant notes, and underline the key action or issues to be delivered. If you are unsure of any detail or objective, always seek clarification to ensure you do not waste your energy on doing the wrong thing. Check the time you have available and always make a plan to complete the task on time by breaking it down into sections and allocating time to each section. At the end, check that your output matches the brief you underlined at the start. In this way you are ensuring you are delivering what is required.

TOP TIPS: Exercises

- Listen carefully and take notes.
- Underline any key actions.
- Always establish what has to be achieved.
- Seek clarification if needed.
- Check the available time.
- Plan what you have to achieve.
- Check your results match the brief.

Individual exercises

For individual exercises, follow all the tips above about staying focused and following a plan – and don't be distracted by the other candidates. Specifically, there's no need to be alarmed by people who complete the task ahead of you; remember, speed of delivery does not mean they are correct! I recall one candidate who completed a 30-minute exercise in 10 minutes. They sat looking at the other candidates with a rather smug look on their face, apparently feeling rather superior for completing the task first, and I am sure some of the other candidates who saw this will have felt intimidated. However, when we looked at this candidate's work, it was of a poor standard and did not address what had been requested. In fact, the only positive we could take from the work was that they had completed the task in the timescale that was requested. Speed means little if the accuracy is poor, and there is very rarely any extra credit given for completing a task early. You have your timescale from your plan and need to work towards it to complete the exercise correctly.

At all stages it is important that you keep a positive attitude about the task you have been set to complete. If you have struggled with an exercise, it can sometimes be hard to remain positive without the collaboration of other candidates to keep you going, but remember it is only one of a series of exercises and you will be given other opportunities to demonstrate your skills later. Everyone will have at least one exercise or task that they are less comfortable with during the event, so do not expect to be great at everything you do: it is unrealistic. Don't forget such shortfalls will be part of an agreed development plan when you join the company.

TOP TIPS: Individual exercises

- Stay positive.
- Outline the objective and plan.
- Check your progress against time.
- Review your final work.

Group exercises

During these exercises you will have to deal with other people and their priorities. You want to be seen as either the leader of the team or a good team player; both roles show off equally valuable and desirable interpersonal skills to the assessors. Whether as team leader or team player, you will at times agree with others and at other times disagree, but it is how you do these things that matter. No company wants someone who agrees all of the time, and they definitely don't want someone who disagrees with everyone, but almost every company wants to hire someone who can agree and disagree graciously. So, you need to be careful how you create the right impression of your approach. Think about these things:

- stay calm, especially when disagreeing, and especially if you feel things are going wrong;
- maintain a 'can do' attitude – be solutions-focused, not problem-focused.

As for all the exercises, it's important to know what has to be achieved in the exercise the team have been allocated. This may mean you are the one to ask for clarification from the briefer; being unafraid to speak up like this is a positive, and keeps the team on track to success. Then, when the team succeeds in the task, your role will be clearly noted by the assessor. You will also be aware of the importance of planning a task – again, don't be afraid to speak up and encourage your group to make a plan. A good way to do this is to suggest to the group that each person should offer their ideas in turn to the group. Some will be willing to do this whilst others will not have any ideas they feel they can share, but by involving people you will show that you can work collaboratively rather than competitively, and will not be seen as a 'dominator'.

However, if you are not successful in getting the team to create a plan do not switch off from the team and their efforts. Remember, stay calm and with a can-do attitude – in other words, remain an active part of the team and commit to the exercise. If you switch off, you risk being seen as petulant because you did not get your own way, even if your way really was the right approach. This is really crucial and often forgotten. Because people see the assessment day as so important, it is easy to forget that making the best of things graciously is a necessary skill in most jobs, so assessors will be looking for it as part of the group tasks.

I was assessing an event for a large organization in the UK. During one group exercise, one candidate took the lead with a full proposal and a series of clear actions to complete the task. They looked so pleased with their input and seemed convinced that their way was the best way; the rest of the group, however, decided to take another course of action.

Instead of assertively trying to persuade the group of the value of their plan, or recognizing the alternative approach and cheerfully supporting the group's decision, the candidate instead told the group that they were wrong and would now fail in the task. They then further said they wanted nothing to do with failure, removed themselves from the group, and watched their efforts without comment.

When the group succeeded with the task, this candidate's only comment was that the group were lucky and should have followed the initial lead. Whether they were right or wrong about the two plans, such an attitude of arrogance and withdrawal did not go down well with the assessors, who were hoping to see good examples of teamwork and problem solving. Regardless of which plan was used, the assessors saw these positive, collaborative behaviours in the whole group – except, of course, the individual who had removed themselves from the process after their idea was not followed. Needless to say, they were not selected for the role. You may be right, but your behaviour has to match your content.

You have started correctly by suggesting a plan; you now need to be prepared to share your ideas freely with the group. Share them with enthusiasm and explain why they will work. Furthermore, you should encourage others to have ideas and listen to these actively. Look for the positives in the ideas and try to develop the correct way forward. When a practical exercise is in full flow, ask others how they are doing and ask if they need any help. This will demonstrate your collaboration skills and show that you are playing an active part in the exercise.

When the exercise is completed it is useful to ask the group how they feel it went and how they think they could improve the output. You can suggest that you are aware that sometimes these exercises are run again. Share your views openly but don't be too critical of individuals. Where you see improvements share them without blaming others.

TOP TIPS: Group exercises

- Stay calm even when things go wrong.
- Develop a can-do approach.
- Share your ideas.
- Involve others in the team.
- Review your final output.
- Stay positive if others are negative.

Repeat exercises

This is a type of exercise that should be seen as distinct from the group exercises. It is a group exercise, but it is one where you now have some relevant experience and know what will work and what needs to improve. Such exercises are used to test whether you can see more than one solution to a problem and can be flexible in your approach. You may be asked to do the exercise using a different method or in a more efficient way, for example, using fewer materials or at a lower cost. It can help to see this as another challenge to demonstrate your talents and tenacity. Let the others know that you are being positive and expect the same from them. You need to adopt a positive approach and ensure you are seen to encourage the rest of the participants.

Such exercises can often bring out a degree of frustration in parts of the team or an individual. This will be shown by their approach and statements like, 'We have just done this so let's just do the same again', or 'Why do we have to do this again?' This is a challenge to the team, as the person is showing they are not on board with the next exercise. At times it is difficult to handle such a situation, but you need to try to get the person working on the task and working with the team. If you fail, you will be credited with trying.

With this exercise you need to be clear about what is expected of the team, and clarify the brief to ensure the efforts of the team are not wasted. Try to ensure your plan is a good attempt to make a difference from the last exercise, although it is useful to review what you have just completed and develop a plan based on that, which also builds in the improvements. At the end of the exercise, if it works, thank the team for their efforts – remember, polite and positive!

TOP TIPS: Repeat exercises

- Get the team on board with the task.
- Develop a new plan – don't be tempted to cut corners.
- Keep everyone involved.
- Review your output against the objective.
- Thank the team at the end.

Difficulties

You will not always succeed with the tasks you are given, perhaps because of the team dynamics, lack of skill in the group, or mistakes being made. These issues can arise in any group or assessment situation. At times, too, the organization may want to deliberately set difficulties in an exercise; this will be their way to identify how candidates cope when things do not go as planned. When these issues arise, remember: stay calm and can-do. You need to show you want to do the task correctly but that you have the calmness not to panic. Panic only causes even more mistakes.

I remember a particular exercise at an assessment event where the resources offered to the group were deliberately limited; however, this was not obvious. For example, a stapler only had 10 staples in it, but most groups assumed it was full and made plans to use rather a lot of staples. This became obvious to one group at the point where they had run out of staples. One person was so upset when they were not given an additional set of staples that they became abusive with the assessor who refused the additional resources, completely missing the point that the group were supposed to manage with what was now available. The angry candidate tried to lead a rebellion with their group, encouraging everyone to refuse to complete the exercise. Only one other person decided to follow this lead. By the end, the rest of the group, who had remained focused and not allowed themselves to be drawn into anger, frustration or refusal to engage, had almost made a success of the exercise – which candidates do you suppose had the most positive results from that exercise?!

When faced with any difficulty, try to overcome it and focus on the issues, not the person. When we make personal attacks on someone, their natural reaction is to fight back. This leads to an argument which in turn takes everyone away from the objective of the exercise. When the discussion gets personal it makes it more difficult for the person to alter their view as it is a personal climb-down that may be interpreted as a weakness, and no one wants to be seen as weak in an assessment process. Therefore, keep away from being personal about any concerns or issues. Always be objective and focused on the task you have been asked to complete.

An unclear brief

The source of most problems or tasks in an assessment event is the briefing of the instructions. Too often they are spoken rather quickly, or the different members of the group will have conflicting ideas and opinions about them. Never allow the briefer to leave the room until you (and the team, if a group task) are clear about what is required to complete the exercise correctly. This may involve you repeating back what you believe is the content of the brief, or asking the person to repeat the instructions again. Don't be afraid to ask; it will be seen as a positive thing, as it makes it clear that you want to do the right task and are prepared to ask questions that are relevant. Remember, if you have only a vague idea of what is required, you have very little chance of success.

The dominator

In group tasks, you can sometimes get a dominator who has all the ideas and does not want to listen to others. It's understandable, perhaps, as everyone is competing for a job and wants to make sure they stand out, but in reality such behaviour has a negative effect on a team, and ultimately is an undesirable trait for hiring organizations. However, candidates often get away with this, because no one wants to tackle them. You can and should stop this approach. If you are able to politely but firmly stop one candidate from dominating the day, you will be seen in a positive light as a person who wants to do the tasks correctly by involving others in the plans and activity.

If you find yourself working with a dominator, you can manage the conversation by asking other individuals if they have any ideas, or by thanking the person for their views while stating that it's always good to have more than one option to consider. By regularly trying to involve the whole team, you are more likely to get the best out of them in the task you all face together. Be aware though – although this kind of behaviour can be very frustrating, don't be tempted to get into an argument with the dominator, as you want to be showing assertive behaviours, not aggressive ones.

Different views

All too often we will be faced with people who have different views to our own. This can be frustrating but it is a situation you have to overcome. When you get to this position it is best to involve the others in the group to decide the best way to move forward. By doing this, the decision is made by the team, and not by two people having an argument. If the decision goes against you, it is advisable to cheerfully state your backing for the group's view and put your energy into the new way forward. This will show that you are a team player and do not moan about any decisions that go against you. Such situations will arise at work regularly, and no organization wants people who cannot support ideas different from their own.

Sometimes you may face not just different ideas, but different attitudes as well – namely, negative attitudes. During one group exercise I observed, the team had to develop a number of solutions in a set period of time. They seemed enthusiastic about the task and started to develop many potential solutions to share with another group who were working independently. This part of the task went well.

However, when it was time to share their views and ideas with the other team they came across a person who seemed to only be capable of telling them that this idea will not work, or they could not see what that idea would do. At first, the team saw this as only a mild setback, but after 10 ideas were pushed away by the same person, the whole team were somewhat deflated. They had put so much effort into the exercise, and one person had killed both their ideas and their enthusiasm.

As the observer, I thought it was strange that no one in the team engaged with the individual to find out why they disagreed or what they would do differently. The team just accepted the person's word – their negative word – without question or explanation. Of course, at the end of the exercise they had no agreed solutions and were unable to deliver the objective.

The whole group knew they should have done something but were obviously unsure what to do. They seemed to be reluctant to challenge each other for fear of being seen as a person who generates conflict; in practice, though, they created the opposite negative impression. By asking the person to explain why they disagreed, they could have developed a better solution. They could have been seen as people who challenge in a positive manner to get to a solution rather than peacekeepers at any price. As it stood, the group had failed to make an impact on the assessors with their performance in the exercise.

From time to time, there may be just one person who sees things differently to the rest of the group. Try to explore why they feel the way they do about their idea, and look for facts and common ground so that you can build some rapport. If they still want their own way, you need to persuade them to come with the majority.

Do not forget that the person may have a different brief to the rest of the group. By identifying common ground and the various differences, we may identify that the briefs are different, and the new or additional information will only enhance the group output.

Varying skill levels

If the team do not have the ideas or the skill to do the task, you need to be seen to be trying to do the best job possible. By recognizing that the task is not going well you can try to guide the team to another course of action. This is often met with, 'We do not have time to change course now'. You can counter that by getting the team to agree that the current situation is not working so you have to try another approach that will at least be correct even if it is not completed.

The employer will recognize that certain skills are not common to everyone taking part, so you need to try and draw out the skills from others in the group. If the skills are not present, the team need to spend more time on planning and preparation to try to overcome the lack of skill. You may not succeed in this task but you can show your tenacity to try and to not give in as well as demonstrate your skills in using relevant process and preparation skills.

Innovator/rebel

There is another person to be on the lookout for in your group – the innovator/rebel. Similar to the dominator, this is a person who thinks they have a great idea that simplifies the exercise. The idea will seem straightforward but on reflection it will breach the standards or constraints of the exercise. The person will not accept this and will cajole the group into following their idea; they are likely to be persuasive but are really only taking an easy way out. You can spot such an idea as it will usually only take five minutes to complete the exercise instead of the 30 minutes allowed. The exercise is 30 minutes long, to allow you time to show how you work, but the innovator/rebel will take that opportunity away from you and the group. The old adage, 'if it is too good to be true it will not be true' is correct in this instance.

I was an assessor once when such a person came up with what they thought was a great idea. The team were tasked with building a tower out of paper that had to stand seven feet tall from the ground. The person had the idea of using one piece of paper and drawing seven feet along the side. They put their idea to the group, who were not sure what to do, but followed their lead.

When the team were told that the structure would fail to meet the standards, not only because it did not meet the spirit of the brief, but also because writing and drawing materials were not included in the allocated resources, the person became abusive and indicated that the assessor was a cheat and did not want the group to succeed. The others in the group were split, with some joining in and others wanting to get back to the brief. Needless to say, the innovator/rebel and the supporters did not make the grade. The group had failed, but they could not see it as they were carried away with the idea of a quick win. Don't be tempted, as it can easily backfire on you.

Use of time

All exercises will have a set time constraint, to give you enough time to complete the task as well as offer consistency between different groups who are set the same task. As we know, it is essential that you plan to use the time you are given in a practical and structured way, but if time gets away from you and you find you have not been monitoring the task's progress against the deadline, don't panic. Take a moment to quickly re-plan the exercise to deliver as many of the requirements as possible; you will achieve partial success and have shown an ability to prioritize, which will be better than just drifting to the end of the exercise having done nothing about the time issue. It's best to keep a regular check on time during exercises, but if that doesn't happen, by calmly and quickly re-prioritizing (with your group if necessary) you will usually overcome any issues arising from losing track of time.

Mistakes

Remember that not everything you are set to achieve will go well. You will almost certainly make mistakes – it's human to do so – but the biggest mistake you can make will be to let your mistakes throw you off and lower your confidence. Don't panic! If you get something wrong, forget an answer, or feel like you've messed up, try to let go and move on quickly. If it's possible, correct what went wrong; if not, don't waste time dwelling on what you cannot change, but keep your focus on the current exercise. You can even sometimes turn a mistake into a positive; for example, during the interview, you can discuss the mistake or exercise that went wrong with your interviewer. You have an opportunity to describe how you would perform differently in the future, why you acted as you did (without excuses, which come off as being defensive, but with a focus on constructive reflection), and why it didn't work. This will demonstrate good intentions, logical thinking, and a mature ability to learn and reflect on your own performance. These are desirable assets in an employee, and from messing up, you have turned it around to show off a strength.

TOP TIPS: Difficulties

- Don't complain, overcome.
- Be seen to tackle difficult people but know when to back away.
- Keep your focus on the brief and what needs to be achieved.
- Re-plan if a task is going wrong.
- Don't worry about mistakes, put them right.
- Focus on the issue, not the person.

At the end

All assessment centres come to an end. You will probably feel relieved and possibly tired. This is normal as you will have been working without much of a break on new exercises that you have never faced before.

Make sure you leave looking positive, with a smile on your face. This leaves a final good impression of you and your performance. Ensure you thank those involved in the team exercises with you. You may not see them again but it demonstrates that you have regarded them as team mates during the event. You also should thank the assessors as you leave. Make them aware you enjoyed the experience and would welcome any relevant feedback at a later stage. They will remember that you want feedback and may prepare for that when entering the decision stage.

As you leave, say goodbye to the receptionist and others you have met during the day if they are seen. Try not to talk to the other candidates about the exercises. Some will want to do this to confirm their views, but it will not help your mood if the views are different and you may spend unnecessary time thinking about who was right. If you have performed to the best of your ability and knowledge you do not need to consider anyone else's views except those of the observers. You don't need this type of frustration. You now need to get away and relax.

Key points to remember

1   Be polite to everyone you meet at the event.

2   You are always being observed.

3   Be positive at all times and offer a structure to the exercise.

4   Take control if the exercise is not going well.

5   Thank everyone at the end before you leave.

11
Gaining feedback after the event

Feedback is one of the most valuable outcomes from an assessment centre. It can offer a practical and independent view of how you work and share your skills with others. Whilst the obvious desired outcome of an assessment centre would be a job offer, in practical terms, honest, pragmatic feedback is probably the more valuable outcome in the long run. Remember, feedback should offer a view of what you do well, as well as what you can do to be even better. It is a major benefit when delivered well.

We often look at feedback as being negative. Perhaps the way we have received it in the past – say, at school – has taught us that receiving a critique is always an unpleasant experience. But let's look at why this may be. When you look back at those negative experiences, you may recall that the communication was very one way, and possibly a surprise at the time, with no chance for preparation on your part. As we saw with the verbal feedback exercises in Chapter 5, truly valuable feedback is a two-way process, and works best when you have prepared for the event and are ready to hear the other person's view. By engaging in the feedback conversation, you will be able to take an active part in the evaluation of your performance, and this can completely change the nature of the experience. When you invest time in an assessment centre, then, it definitely makes sense to ask for relevant feedback about your performance, to help you develop your skills in the future and perform better in other assessment events.

Most feedback you receive will have a structure to it. It will usually focus on the positive areas first, then the improvement areas, with relevant examples of your performance for both. The person giving the feedback will ask for your views at various stages to ensure there is harmony of views, usually after every major section. The final stage will be to discuss how to maintain the good areas and make the improvements that are required. You will want to know specifically how you could perform better at future events, to assist you in your job search and help build your confidence for any future assessments you encounter.

Preparation

We need to look at how to get the best out of this process in order to help you enhance your skills for the future. This requires an element of pre-work on your part; if such work is not completed, you are returning to the ineffective one-way feedback process you have encountered in the past. You can prepare by spending time reflecting on the assessment event. Concentrate on each exercise one at a time and consider how you performed; look at what skills you employed and any areas in which you encountered difficulty. Was the difficulty because of your lack of skills or knowledge, or was it down to the technicality of the brief?

The only way to review the assessment process is with total honesty about yourself. Try to only focus on what you did and what you could have done. Resist the temptation to focus on the actions or input of others, as this will get you nowhere when the point is to reflect on you.

Here is a useful template to help you prepare for post-assessment centre feedback. Take your time when filling it out and look at every exercise in turn. Do not rush, as it will serve as the basis for taking part in any feedback you receive from the organization. It's best to try to complete it as soon as possible after the event; this way, your memory will be fresh and you will miss very little of the detail. If you wait until the night before the feedback, you will likely miss a lot.

HOW DO YOU RATE YOUR PERFORMANCE?

1 Which exercises worked well and why?

2 What would you do differently in the exercises?

3 Which exercises went not so well and why?

4 What would you do differently in the exercises?

5 What are your strengths?

Skill	Knowledge

6 What are your improvement areas?

Skill	Knowledge

7 What development would you like in order to enhance your performance?

One good way to ensure you miss nothing is to complete the questionnaire and put it away for a few days. Revisit your work a few days later and re-read the content – you will be amazed at how much extra you will be able to add to the notes, as your subconscious reflects while you are concentrating on other things.

Once you have completed the questionnaire, you need to make the organization aware that you are seeking feedback from the event. You can do this by e-mail or a phone call, where you also need to give an indication of the kind of feedback you are looking for. Many organizations will offer vague platitudes about finding a more qualified candidate; this may be true, and may even make you feel better, but it does not help you going forward as it has offered no specific information on what you need to improve and what you should continue doing. It is useful, then, to outline what you are asking for in advance. Be specific! You may also like to get the feedback from a person who was an observer at the event. Whilst you cannot demand too much time or information, you can certainly ask for what you want.

The following list can be used as a guide or a template in asking for specific feedback, but you should absolutely feel free to ask for any additional information that may have come from the process. If you do not ask, you will not receive. You can ask for feedback roughly one week after the event, or when the hiring decision has been made.

WHAT FEEDBACK DO YOU REQUIRE?

1 An outline of how you performed against each of the competencies with examples from exercises.

2 What are seen as my key strengths?

3 How can I improve in the future?

4 Any recommendations to develop my improvement areas?

5 An outline of your test results.

6 A copy of your personality profile.

Remember, you will still need feedback even if you have been selected for the role. If you were selected, then this feedback will help you to settle into the job more quickly and can be the basis of a solid action plan for your orientation into the new role. You are more likely to get a face-to-face session with the company if you were offered the role, but be aware that in some cases they may ask you to wait until you have joined the company and use the information as part of your induction.

The feedback

Most companies will want to offer you one-way feedback, as this is quicker and uses fewer resources. A lot of people just accept that this is the way feedback is given by organizations, but if you make it clear you want a discussion, this will help you engage with the feedback and perform better in the future. You need to be polite in all your dealings with the organization as it will get you more rounded and detailed feedback. There are instances where the person who has sought feedback has gained a job offer because they left a good impression and a suitable job had arisen by the time of feedback.

Most feedback will not involve a face-to-face meeting. However, if you do get offered such a meeting, it is best to accept, as this gives you another opportunity to impress the organization. You need to take as much care of your appearance for the face-to-face meeting as you did when attending the assessment event. This is still a formal meeting and should be used to try to impress the organization.

All feedback sessions will have a form of introduction to the process. This may be in the form of an informal section at the start of a discussion or greeting-type pleasantries. This is to allow both parties to settle into the feedback mode. Be prepared for this and accept that it will be useful. If you get straight into the feedback, you will have little or no rapport with the person and this can lead to a feeling that the feedback is no more than a process rather than a relevant discussion.

Written feedback

Most feedback is either given in a written format or via a phone call. The written feedback is of course that one-way communication we want to avoid, so you should be prepared to ask for a discussion about the report. Make it clear you do not disagree with the findings, you only want more details. This makes it more likely you will get the discussion. If you appear to disagree with the findings, most organizations will reject the plea for more information in order to avoid conflict.

Before you have the discussion, go through the written report and outline what you agree with and what you want further details on. This allows you to be in control of the information you require. If you just listen to the feedback and chip in when you feel you should, you will get little or no specific information.

The test results are an area you want to explore. You want to know how well you did against the norm group they were measured against; in this way you will know how well you can perform in the future. It is also a good idea to explore how much these tests count in the overall decision.

Similarly, the personality questionnaire feedback is useful. This will be delivered either as a two-way discussion about personality traits or as a report. If it is a discussion, you can explore and explain your views. If it is a report, you may want to have a separate discussion about the profile. Again, make it clear you do not disagree with the results, but that you want to know more about how these traits impact on the role.

Verbal feedback

This is a good method of feedback as it offers you the opportunity to take part in a conversation or a discussion. That means you can find out more about how you performed and how you can make improvements in the future. There are some possible pitfalls, though; you should not be tempted to enter into a heated discussion, or to refuse to either believe or listen to the other party. Hearing feedback, as we have discussed, can be potentially stressful, but if you cause conflict over the feedback you will not get very far, as the other person will be more guarded about their views and may even terminate the discussion. You lose out on two accounts: first, you get little information, and second, you have represented yourself badly and are unlikely to be considered for future roles.

I had one individual ask for feedback after an assessment centre where they had not been successful in gaining the job. They had asked for personal feedback by telephone on a specific date and time – all very good so far. The person's performance at the event was not outstanding and some of their skills were well below what was expected for entry into the role. This should have been a straightforward feedback session as there were many facts and examples of their performance.

The feedback started well, with pleasant introductions by both parties and an explanation of the feedback process from me. The person said they wanted the feedback in order to improve in the future, especially if they faced an assessment event again, so I started by asking the person how they believed they had performed and what they would do differently. The reply was strange as they believed they were the best candidate and would change nothing except the assessors who they believed could not see their skills. We talked about each exercise and the person could not see how an assessor could identify faults that were not there. When presented with examples of their performance, they either said that it was not true or gave an excuse for their actions.

The conversation lasted over an hour and was painful at times as the person refused to accept any constructive criticism, only appearing to accept the positive feedback they were given. At the end, I asked what they had learned about themselves and all they could say was that they were better than the other candidates and would have been a perfect fit for the role. They had nothing to improve and had found the feedback unhelpful. I thanked the person and wished them well. I am sure they still think they are great – let's hope whoever they work for has the same view!

Unlike the difficult person from this story, if you disagree with something, the best way to deal with it is to ask for more information about the view that was expressed. This will give you a more rounded view of the information. Keep an open mind about the feedback; remember, the provider gains no benefit out of giving poor information that is not based on facts, so it's possible you will hear something that will help you, and you then will get assistance with how to improve. If you totally disagree with some of the feedback – even after asking for more information – leave that area until the end. In order to maintain the flow of the other person's information and get the total picture, you should just listen carefully to the other points and ask for additional information when appropriate. If you spoil the flow, the feedback may become stilted as the other person could be defensive. This will not help your future development.

Then, near the end of the conversation, you can raise the area you disagree with. Some suggested phrasing might be: 'I agree with all of the feedback you have given, it was most useful, thank you. The one area I cannot see in the same way is X. The reason for that is Y, how do you see that?' This approach should get a good response. Acknowledging that you agree with most of what has been said keeps a positive atmosphere to the discussion, so you will appear positive and inquisitive but not antagonistic.

Face to face

This is not a normal feedback method adopted by most companies as they find the first two methods less time-consuming. If you are invited to discuss feedback face to face, you need to be well prepared for the views that may be expressed. You will probably go through a similar model to that shown in Table 11.1 when discussing your performance; as you can see, you will need to have your own views and examples of your performance ready to share with the other person.

Table 11.1 Feedback process

You	Organization
	Good points
Your views	
	Improvements
Your views	
	How to improve
	Test and personality profile
Your views	

The key to such a meeting is to start and stay in a calm mood, and listen carefully to what is said. Make notes as you go and make appropriate comments about the feedback you have been given. Where necessary, as in the other forms of feedback, ask for more details or examples so that you can understand the points being made. Because a face-to-face meeting is more in-depth and represents more investment of time and resources on behalf of both parties, you may wish

Table 11.2 Feedback analysis

Competency area	Your views	Feedback
Leadership		
Teamwork		
Problem analysis		
Problem solving		
Decision making		
Influencing		
Interpersonal skills		
Creativity		
Tenacity		
Flexibility		
Verbal communication		
Written communication		
Planning and organizing		
Business acumen		
Skills		
Numeric		
Data analysis		
Verbal reasoning		

to do more preparation. A good way to do this is to use Table 11.2 to outline your views against a number of relevant competency areas. This may take some time, but will relate to the preparation you have done using the questionnaire form earlier in the chapter; by looking at the competencies you will be talking the language of the assessors.

As you can see, there is space for you to then note the feedback points being made against each competency as they are outlined, which will help you structure the meeting; if the feedback and your views are the same, you can tick the area as agreed, and you may not want to spend so much time on these areas. You will be able to clearly see which areas have an element of disagreement, and can pursue these by asking for more examples or information from the person delivering the feedback. This will help you keep track of the feedback you have received. It is also worth asking how they feel any areas of improvement can be bridged in the future. This will lead to a positive discussion about your improvements that should be useful in your development.

If there is a gap in your feedback analysis you can ask for the person's view of that specific competency to give you a more rounded view, which would not have been possible without the preparation. The purpose of this template, and the others in this chapter, is to ensure you maximize the feedback areas and have relevant examples of your performance so that these can be readily discussed.

Although I have recommended this model for use in a face-to-face meeting, you can use it to track any method of feedback. It will assist you in keeping the feedback output in line with your requirements, and in showing that you have prepared well to enter into a positive and structured discussion. This will enhance the view the organization has of you as a potential recruit for any future roles (or even the same role if a decision has yet to be made). Regardless, the outputs will enhance your confidence in future dealings with organizations.

The end

At the end of any feedback it is useful to summarize what has been said. You can only do this by taking good notes as you go through, perhaps by using the feedback analysis template. The summary can be taken directly from the notes; you can outline the areas of agreement and strengths, and any areas where there is room for improvement.

When you have summarized, ask the other person if they agree with the summary or would like to comment. Listen carefully to the comments and reply if necessary. You need to be focused on what they say rather than considering your reply; you can develop a suitable reply when they have finished speaking.

The final act is to thank the person for their time and concern. Let them know you have appreciated their efforts – remember, they did not owe you this feedback, and it would have been easier for them to simply send a rejection, or wait until your first day if you were selected for the role. If you weren't, you could add that you would still like to work for the organization if a suitable role came up in the future. This leaves a positive impression that could lead to further contact.

If the contact has been by e-mail or letter, send a positive response and again, ensure you take the time to thank the person for the time spent on the feedback. Make sure they know you have valued the feedback and will act on it in the future. These things take very little time, but not only are they polite, they will keep you positively in the mind of the organization should any roles happen to become vacant in the future. You will be surprised how many people gain job offers after they have not been appointed at an assessment centre; after all the assessment processes you have gone through they know rather a lot about you and will be able to determine if you are a good fit for most roles, even a new vacancy that was not available at the time of the assessment event.

Key points to remember

1 You are entitled to ask for feedback with the time and effort you have devoted to this process.

2 Reflect honestly on how you performed at the event.

3 List the areas of feedback you require before you contact the organization.

4 Listen with an open mind to the feedback you receive and take relevant notes.

5 Thank the person for taking the time to deliver the feedback.

Conclusions

Thank you for the time you have spent reading this book; I hope you have found the content both practical and useful. I hope that now, when you face your next assessment centre, you will feel more confident about the process and how to perform effectively on the day of the event.

You need to remember that most organizations are using this process as an aid to developing even better recruitment decisions. Whilst a traditional interview will still be used by some organizations, there is a movement towards a more robust process that will allow the candidate to demonstrate their skills and behaviours whilst being observed by a trained assessor. Ultimately, organizations are looking for the best person for a job, and they want that person to settle into the role quickly and be able to demonstrate their usefulness to their peers. By going through the assessment process you will have a complete development plan to assist you in the settling-in period in the new job if you are successful. You will know by now that organizations are looking for skills, knowledge and behaviours when they recruit, and this development plan will be used to fill in the gaps in areas that are important to the new role. Being observed and going through such in-depth exercises may at first seem like a strange situation, but you will in a very short period of time forget you are being observed, so the assessor will see the real you.

We've looked at some potential mistakes and fears, and hopefully by now you feel equipped to handle the day whatever happens. Remember, the most unforgivable mistake you can make is not being prepared for an assessment centre. In almost every chapter, we have looked at how preparation will lead directly to a boost in confidence and better performance when you attend the event; this confidence will make you look the part and put you ahead of those who have not bothered. You can boost your confidence levels even higher by trying some of the exercises in the book, giving yourself a head start on other candidates and at the same time enhancing your confidence and style of delivery. If you have done all of these exercises and got some helpful feedback from friends or trusted colleagues, and you want to practise some more, you can also go online to find suitable examples of exercises and psychometric tests. Trying some of SHL's tests (referred to in Chapter 8), which are available from their website, will further enhance your preparation.

I am sure you will continue to put every relevant effort into your assessment centre and impress the assessors with your skills, but remember too that organizations are just as interested in the process you use as the results you obtain. It is possible to impress an assessor by doing the right thing and failing to complete the task. Obviously, it is best to achieve both, but the process you follow is the most important area for the organization, as they are able to see that you work in a structured manner.

In the introduction, I spoke about my first experience of an assessment centre – how anxious I was, and how unsure of what was coming. What made me feel confident then was, as I said, the calm, thorough and clear explanation of what I was about to face. I hope that this book has done the same for you! Just knowing how these events work, what the purpose is behind them, and what the employer is looking for will aid your confidence building. As we have seen, any relevant preparation you do in advance of your assessment centre will be time well spent, as it will enable you to perform better and to your full potential

I will leave you with this story from my own experience, since I have applied the techniques described in the book myself. A number of years ago, I really wanted a specific job with a major brewing company. This was a job I had always wanted, and I knew it was unlikely to come on the market again in the near future. I applied, and found out that an assessment centre would be a part of the recruitment process. Just like I have outlined in the chapters here, I studied the job description and asked to see the company competence framework. From this I was able to predict the likely types of tools they would employ during the assessment day, and practise the exercises and interview techniques that were likely to come up.

Before the event, I was nervous, but due to the research and practice I had done with my family and friends, I was able to go into the day with an inner calm and confidence. The event was a challenge, but because of my preparation, it was not stressful. Most of what I researched happened, although there were of course one or two surprises, as there always are, but the main thing is that I got the job and had a number of rewarding years at the company in a role that lived up to my expectations. It goes to show that if you are prepared, you will be more confident and therefore more likely to succeed. I wish you the best of luck in your encounters with assessment centres – the rest is up to you!

APPENDIX 1
Model answer for identifying skills from a job description

You need to spend some time looking at the skills required to successfully complete the requirements of the role, as this will help you identify any skills you need to develop, and assist you in preparing for the assessment event by completing some of the exercises in the book.

In this model answer to the exercise on page 15, you can clearly see that various tasks are completed successfully by using different skills (see Table App 1.1). Where you see these tasks in the job description, you need to consider what skills you have that will help you achieve these tasks. This will show you the skills that will be measured during the assessment. You will now be able to practise these skills prior to the event.

Table App 1.1 Skills identification

Tasks	Skills
Achieve results	Tenacity and planning
Ability to work with others	Interpersonal skills
Pass on information	Verbal and written skills
Decisive action	Problem solving and decision making
Disciplined approach to work	Plan and organize
Initiative	Problem solving and creativity
Take responsibility for work area and team	Leadership and teamwork

APPENDIX 2
Model answer for written report 1

Here is a model-type answer to the report exercise in Chapter 5 using the Introduction, Main Points and Summary model. This is for a made-up Operations Manager job but will demonstrate how the model operates and what should be included at each stage. It also demonstrates the indenting process for each section in order to create a more readable report.

Induction programme for A. Candidate, 3 May 20xx

1.0 Introduction

This report is required to outline a practical induction programme for myself as a potential new employee (Operations Manager) in the organization. I have recently attended an assessment event which lasted two days.

The assessment event was structured to address the key skills and competencies required to deliver the role of operations manager within the organization. A series of relevant exercises were used which included reports, presentations and prioritization exercises.

The results of these exercises have been used to devise an induction programme that will enable me as the successful candidate to settle into the new role both quickly and effectively and will enable me to deliver effective results within the new role.

2.0 Induction content (main body)

This report will outline the required output of the induction programme for the new employee. It will take account of their current skill level and identified development needs.

2.1 Company history

I had completed a good deal of research about the company which was demonstrated by the relevant content of my reports and presentations. I feel I will need a more specific input from the organization about the history that is relevant to the operations function. This will include why the organization uses the systems that are employed and any future plans for the further development of the operation. Time should also be spent discussing the various key accounts and customers as well as their specific requirements of the operations function.

This content should be delivered by the Operations Director, who will be able to give a good explanation of the company history and where the operations function fits with the corporate objectives. The output from this session will enable me as a new recruit to be able to identify why we take certain actions as well as establish which customers make the greatest impact on the corporate objectives.

2.2 Department structure

I will also need to become familiar with the current structure of the department and any planned future changes. This will enable me to more rapidly absorb how the department operates and the amount of manpower that is available. Time will need to be spent looking at each section and what they are expected to achieve.

The individuals who hold each role should be discussed to ensure there is a clear understanding of what each person contributes to the overall goals. Time should be spent explaining the reasons for each role and how they have developed over the last few years. This will help when I am introduced to the new team as I will be familiar with the names as well as what each person's role is in the organization. I would propose that I am given a guided tour of the department where I can see the layout as well as meet the key players in the department.

At a later date I can be introduced to all of the team both as a total team and then individually. This section of the induction can be delivered by either the Operations Director or the previous job holder.

2.3 Department focus

When settling into any new role, it is essential that any new employee is made familiar with not only the corporate objectives but also the department objectives. This will enable me to identify where the department can support the organization's goals. I will need to be shown how the department focus was developed as well as their role in the delivery of the focus so that I can see where current priorities have developed.

Time should be spent discussing how the main focus will be delivered and how each person in the department can impact that focus. By the end of this session I will be able to identify a number of key activities that will enable me to contribute more effectively to the future of the organization. This session is best delivered by the Operations Director or the CEO.

2.4 Operations Manager role

An explanation and discussion about the new role is probably the most important aspect of the induction for any new recruit and this role is no different, as it should outline what is expected of the person and how they will be measured. This has been part of the recruitment process but still needs to be included as part of the induction to ensure there is clarity about what is expected of me in the new role.

Time needs to be spent looking at the key aspects of the job and what tasks make the greatest difference to the efficiency of the organization. This will enable me to be able to identify the key result areas and priorities of the role. I will therefore be able to identify how I will be measured in the role and decide which of the sections of the new team will add the most value.

This section of the induction will need to be very practical and involving to ensure I have a clear idea of the impact the role will have on the new team and the organization. When you are clear about these issues you are more able to identify priorities and overcome strategic decisions. This section should be delivered by the Operations Director.

3.0 *Summary*

It is proposed to have a practical approach to my induction as the new Operations Manager. The specific areas of induction have been identified by a thorough assessment process over two days.

The induction process will need to include:

1 company history;

2 department structure;

3 department focus;

4 role of Operations Manager.

The above areas will be delivered in the main by the Operations Director.

APPENDIX 3
Model answer for written report 2

Here is a model type answer for a written report using the C3PO format. This will demonstrate how to use each of the five sections as part of the report. It demonstrates the use of the indenting system for the sections of the report, which is based on a fictitious company that makes computer games. The content, problems and solutions are neither relevant nor descriptive of the industry but have simply been developed to show how to utilize the report format.

Company problems and solutions:
A. Candidate, 27 April 20xx

1.0 Current situation

The organization Bay Games has been in existence for 10 years and is fairly well established in the computer games market. This market has a sales revenue worldwide of £2 billion per year, and Bay Games has an annual revenue of £200 million.

There is a range of current products that sell well and are part of a franchise linked to a series of movies. Each year the organization is tasked with bringing two major new products to the market. In the past two years this has proved very difficult but has been achieved.

The games that are linked to the movies are selling well. However, the new products have struggled to find a place in this very competitive market. The games seem to be mainly aimed at a male market, which is only 50 per cent of the current market. No game has appealed to the female market.

2.0 Problems faced

2.1 Competition for staff

It is very difficult to find good games engineers and developers as this is a tight market with new entrants each year, and the scarce resource tends to move between organizations every three years. The competition for talent has led to wage increases and even higher labour turnover over the last 12 months.

2.2 Workforce composition

The organization has a diverse workforce but this is not represented in the game developer role. It is believed that this has led to the new games being male-oriented, meaning that the organization is missing out on half its potential market. Everyone is seen as a valuable asset to the organization but this has not prevented a diverse workforce in all areas.

2.3 Game reviews

Most new games are being reviewed as being formulaic and predictable by the influencers of the market. There is seen to be a lack of new ideas and character diversity. This is seen as a major reason why some games have failed to make the expected impact on the market.

3.0 Possible solutions

3.1 Do nothing

Doing nothing is a consideration. The organization is doing well and will continue to do so for the foreseeable future by appealing to its core buyers. The downside of this approach is that the organization will be seen as not responding to the marketplace and may even be seen as a dinosaur. This would hasten any demise as the majority of gamers want to be seen as cutting-edge people.

3.2 University twins

One method of gaining good staff in the future would be to form good links with the universities that provide the best talent. These ties will help promote the organization as a front-runner in the games industry. This approach will cost both time and effort on the part of the company, but this will be repaid if there is a steady stream of good talent brought into the company. Even if the approach fails, it will have promoted the company brand, which may help future recruitment.

3.3 Internal diversity approach

The company can do more with the talent it has within the organization. It needs to promote the role of female developers and encourage all developers to take a more diverse approach to the games being actively developed. This will widen the appeal of the new games in the current marketplace. It will demonstrate to the key players that the company is moving forward and has changed its approach. This will lead to better reviews and therefore more sales.

3.4 School visits

One source of new talent is to identify the raw talent in its early stages and offer such people an apprenticeship route into their career. You will only find this talent by being involved in schools, perhaps by arranging visits to the company studios and involving groups in developing their skills. This will act as a shop window for talent as well as showing that the games industry is a good employer that should be considered as a career.

You may find that some of the talent wants to go through university, but this can be accommodated by keeping in touch with them and offering holiday work or assignments.

4.0 *Proposed actions*

There are two main areas that can be applied immediately and can yield quick results. The internal diversity approach can be implemented at once; it may take time to get results but the quicker you start the quicker it will happen. This involves asking for more diverse games from all involved and also looking to gain more female games developers.

Ties with universities can be implemented immediately but will take some time to bring results. Speaking to recent graduates can help with gaining access to their old universities.

The use of school visits can commence quickly but will take more time before the results can be seen. By taking a three-pronged approach we will get short- and long-term success.

5.0 Overview

This is a difficult time for the games industry due to the scarcity of talent, which will only get worse as competition increases. The company needs to do something about this to ensure its future success. The new games it produces are seen to be either too similar to the established games or do not appeal to a diverse audience.

Any approach that is taken needs to be well considered and have a positive effect on the organization. However, action needs to be rapid and targeted to gain short-term as well as long-term results. It is proposed to take three key actions to address the problems:

1 develop a diverse approach to the development of the new games;

2 create more effective links with universities;

3 develop relevant school visits to attract future talent.

It is believed these three actions will be cost-effective and will help promote the brand to new gamers as well as attract the necessary talent to the organization.

APPENDIX 4
Presentation planning template

Outlined overleaf is a typical format you can use when presenting information to a group of people. The layout is developed to ensure you are aware of all the items you can include. You can use this either as a starting point for developing a presentation or use this document as a template, filling in the gaps. The Introduction section shows what you need to include so that the audience have been greeted, know who you are and how long you will speak for.

By giving an overview of what you will say you will be able to generate interest. A good way to do this is with a hook, which may be a simple but memorable fact or a relevant short story.

The rest of the sections should be populated by the content of the talk. Some people use this as a template and also as a prompt or notes for their presentation to ensure they do not stray from the key points.

Introduction

Greeting	Good morning/afternoon
I am	(Name)
Hook	
I will talk about	(Title)

This will consist of   1. ....

                          2. ....

                          3. ....

I will talk for approximately .... (Minutes)

You can ask questions .... (When)

Main Body

	Back-up data	Aid
1 Main point		
2 Main point		
3 Main point		

Summary

We have looked at   1. ....

                     2. ....

                     3. ....

You can see that	(Conclusion)
What you need to do	(Action if appropriate)
Any questions	

Thank you for your time.

APPENDIX 5
Example of presentation feedback using POOSA

'I will give you some feedback about how I observed your presentation. We will look at the positive areas and how to maintain these in the future. We will then look at what I observed that can be improved, and I will seek your views about the feedback. We can then look at developing solutions to the improvement areas and identify an action plan for use in future presentations. Feel free to take part at any time during our discussion. How do you feel about that?'

Take answers and reply accordingly

Introduction stage: You can see that this example candidate has taken some time to make their person feel at ease by explaining what form the conversation will take. They have checked in with their person, giving them an opportunity to express any concerns.

'The presentation went well and seemed to be addressing most of the areas of the brief. I especially liked your opening, which got a lot of involvement from the audience. You seemed to lay out your key points in a logical sequence that made it easy to follow.

'The visual aids that you used were clear to see and had the right amount of detail to retain interest whilst not being too overpowering on detail. The slide that showed the key problems was a good example of this, as it had only three lines with a word on each. Those words were easy to follow and were supportive of your verbal points.

'The structure you used was again easy to follow. You used the introduction, main points and summary approach, which seemed to fit your content well.

'Your delivery sounded confident as your voice stressed the key points effectively. This in turn helped to keep attention on the content. The content was appropriate for the title and the brief you were given.

'Does that seem fair?'

Listen to and discuss replies

Positive impact: Here we see that our candidate has started with the positives. Each point is detailed and specific – they have given clear reasons why they thought a feature was effective, rather than just saying that they liked it. Again, they have given their person an opportunity to respond to the feedback, allowing a conversation to happen and helping the person feel involved. This helps to create rapport.

'Let us now look at the areas that needed to improve. There are only two of these and I am sure you will be able to solve these in the future.

'During the presentation you spent at least 80 per cent of the time looking at the screen. This makes it hard to see the audience reaction and also to create rapport.

'You also tended to get to the main points without really outlining what you would do and how the presentation would evolve. This made it difficult to keep up with your first point and made me unsure where the presentation was going.

'How do you see that?'

Respond to issues raised

Observed improvements and opinion: Our example candidate has remained matter-of-fact with the points to improve. They remained encouraging – highlighting that there wasn't much to improve and expressing confidence in their person's ability to improve. The points themselves are, like the positives, very specific, outlining the impact of each point and explaining why these improvements are necessary. Once again, they have directly involved their person in the conversation by asking for a response, effectively merging both 'O's' of the POOSA model.

'So how do you think you can overcome these points in the future?'

Listen to views and reply when necessary

Opinion and solution: Our candidate now gives their person the floor. You can see that the suggestions for solutions should come from the person themselves, and haven't been dictated by our candidate. Our candidate has also extended the 'Opinion' stage a little, really giving their person a chance to be active in the discussion.

'Let's put an action plan together for your next presentation. We will look at the actions you will take, how they will happen and when.'

Summary of action plan

Action plan: Now our example candidate has retaken control of the discussion and has given their person a clear structure to focus on concrete improvements. They haven't left their person with a vague sense of needing to improve but not knowing how.

'Thanks for your input into the feedback. It made the process both worthwhile and positive. Good luck with your next presentation. I am sure you will make a great impact by using the action plan to remind yourself of the improvements.'

Summary: Our candidate keeps the mood positive, thanking their person for taking an active role. Everyone leaves feeling good!

APPENDIX 6
Model answer for in-tray prioritization exercise

It is important to understand how to use the grid format for prioritizing exercises. You need to look at each item and establish first whether is it within your role description or if it belongs to someone else. You then need to establish how much of a priority the item is to the organization. Using the grid, you can establish your priorities by looking at what is furthest from the intersection of the axes.

Looking at the list on pages 89–91, you can apply the grid to this workload. It can help you arrive at a rank order; then you can assign the details about what you would do and how you would do it. Figure App 6.1 is an example of a how this grid might look; as you can see, this is a dynamic chart and you will make various changes as you look at the items. These answers will be different for different organizations, but the 'Do Now' area will not change, as these are the key items to being effective.

As you can see, then, there are very few items that need your immediate attention. Even the phone call (15) can be returned later. There are many tasks that can be delegated, for example, 16 (mail room) and 4 (cartridge). Most items, such as 5, 6, 10, and 14, can wait for your return. A simple e-mail will keep people in the loop and let them know that you will address these issues later.

Item 3 has an impact on the organization so should be addressed. However, you do not have the time to do this and you cannot delegate this to a staff member. You could delegate it to your manager when they return later in the week.

Figure App 6.1 Model answer for grid method prioritization

You will need to deal with number 17 as a priority as it will impact on your team. This can be delegated to a team member to brief the team next Monday. Items 7, 8 and 9 need to be addressed today and are a priority. The new trainee will need to be given to a team member to maintain a good induction and impression of the company. You can deal with the day off request (8) by looking at the manpower for the day.

The grievance (9) cannot be heard in the time available, but you can establish if it is important. If it is, you can delegate the issue to your manager. If it can wait, you can deal with it on your return.

Numbers 18 and 19 are good examples of very low-priority items that have no impact on the business in the short term. Item 19 is a personal issue and can be done any time, whilst item 18 (the staff social outing) can be delegated to a team member.

INDEX

Note: Numbers within main headings are filed as spelt out. Acronyms are filed as presented. Page locators in *italics* denote information contained within a Figure or Table.